"*Special Grace* paints a loving and ho[...]irky' kids. As her story unfolds, she make[...]ges caregiving families face. Even on Sun[...] .y on Sundays. With humor and grace, Evans describes obstacles that make worshiping as a family impossible much of the time. Rather than railing against God or blaming the church, she turns to prayer. In so doing, she demonstrates how to tell God how we feel and ask for what we need. She encourages us to lift up to him those situations unique to special-needs and disability parents. Her prayers provide families with a road map back to hope, strength, and endurance through Christ. I love *Special Grace* and its prayers; I think you will too."

Jolene Philo, national speaker and coauthor with Gary Chapman of *Sharing Love Abundantly in Special Needs Families*

"Elrena Evans has done remarkable things with this short volume of Bible verses, vignettes, and prayers related to almost any aspect of being the parent of a child with disabilities. Her authenticity and honesty shine through in ways that feel real—sometimes raw and sometimes funny. Parents can no doubt find themselves in multiple stories and prayers. By offering her family's experiences and feelings in short, poignant prayers, Evans is shining a light on the ways that faith and spirituality permeate the lives of people with disabilities and their families. A pastor or priest seeking to understand families and those dimensions of their lives just might find this an excellent resource that also indirectly points to the ways they and their faith communities might journey with and support these families. It is a book of stories and prayers; it will also preach."

Bill Gaventa, founder and director emeritus of the Institute on Theology and Disability

"Elrena Evans offers parents of kids with special needs a modern-day Psalter. With humor and poignant storytelling, wit and raw honesty, she tells us the hard and hopeful story of her own home life, and she equips us with prayers for every possible moment of grief, thanksgiving, wonder, and need. I'm so thankful this book is in the world."

Amy Julia Becker, author of *White Picket Fences* and *A Good and Perfect Gift*

"Elrena Evans distills her own heart-rending experiences as a special-needs parent into gritty prayers for those who are tired beyond words. Her raw, confessional book of prayers is a beacon of light, truth, and encouragement for those who are in the atypical, neurodivergent trenches."

Tammy Perlmutter, founder and curator of *The Mudroom*

"The stories in *Special Grace* are so relatable that I could laugh and tear up while reading the same page. Not only do we have similar, quirky families, we also have the same faith—and it's that faith that gets us through the hardest days on this parenting journey. I am so thankful to have Elrena Evans's guiding prayers for everything from adjusting to a new medicine to how to respond to less-than-kind comments from strangers. This book is one I'll pick up again and again!"

Sandra Peoples, author of *Unexpected Blessings: The Joys & Possibilities of Life in a Special-Needs Family*

"Some parents utter constant SOS prayers; others are too overwhelmed for words. But every parent navigating an uncommon journey with their child will resonate with the universal struggles and supplications found in *Special Grace*. For the maddening, mysterious, and mundane moments when we find it hard to pray or give thanks in all circumstances, Elrena Evans gets it and has partnered with the Holy Spirit to intercede on our behalf with hope and humor."

Diane Dokko Kim, author of *Unbroken Faith: Spiritual Recovery for the Special-Needs Parent*

"In *Special Grace*, Elrena Evans pulls back the curtain and invites us into the real-life experiences of a parent of children with special needs. Connecting with other exhausted parents, she gently leads them, through prayer, into the presence of the Father to receive his sustaining grace for their journey. A must-read for any parent of a child considered atypical by the world."

Matthew S. Stanford, author of *Grace for the Children: Finding Hope in the Midst of Child and Adolescent Mental Illness*

ELRENA EVANS

FOREWORD BY
JONI EARECKSON TADA

Special Grace

PRAYERS *and*
REFLECTIONS
for FAMILIES
with
SPECIAL NEEDS

An imprint of InterVarsity Press
Downers Grove, Illinois

CONTENTS

FOREWORD: BEFORE YOU BEGIN . . .
BY JONI EARECKSON TADA | 1

INTRODUCTION | 5

1. BEGINNINGS | 9
The Diagnosis 11
Prayers 16

2. FAMILY LIFE | 21
The Do-Over 23
Prayers 30

3. SCHOOL | 39
The Substitute Teacher Problem 41
Prayers 46

4. PUBLIC LIFE | 53
Sunday Morning Minecraft 55
Prayers 60

5. CHANGES | 67
Jumping Out the Window 69
Prayers 74

6. SEASONS OF THE YEAR | 79
The Corn Maze 81
Prayers 86

7. THANKSGIVINGS | 93
Harry Potter Goes to Church 95
Prayers 102

OTHER PRAYERS | 108

ACKNOWLEDGMENTS | 113   LIST OF PRAYERS | 117

BEFORE YOU BEGIN . . .

Joni Eareckson Tada

*B*eautiful, the mess we are. The honest cries of breaking hearts are better than a Hallelujah sometimes."

Long ago, these lyrics of a popular song provided comfort when I was overwhelmed by the rigors of treatment for stage 3 cancer. The song "Better Than a Hallelujah" was raw and visceral. The idea that God readily responds to honest cries of breaking hearts soothed my weary soul like nothing else.

I thought of this song when I read the book you are holding in your hands. Its stories, insights, and prayers that flow from page to page are raw and visceral and, oh, so gut-wrenchingly real. And I love it.

If you live with disability as I do, you, too, will love *Special Grace*. The rigors of living with disability in your family has honed your instincts about what is real, and what is not . . . about what comforts and what does not. You are able to spot well-meaning platitudes that simply do not touch the problem where it hurts—and that's in the gut and in the heart. As a parent of a child with special needs, it's where you live every day.

So does Elrena Evans, the author of this inspired volume. Yes, she is a skilled and gifted writer, but preeminently, she is one tiger-of-a-special-needs mom. With each story, you will resonate with the bruises and wounds, as well as the joys and victories of this mother. Here is a woman who loves her family. And her God.

And she longs to pass on the encouragement to you. Elrena's family stories—and her accompanying insights—are like a tuning fork that strikes a familiar chord in your bruised heart. I am especially grateful for the many—here comes that word again—visceral prayers she offers. Prayers that will help you wisely intercede for yourself, your spouse, and for your special-needs child and his or her siblings.

I shared *Special Grace* with my friend Kristen, a mother of three children with disabilities. She wrote, "Joni, I can't tell you how many times I've teetered on the edge, desperate and wholly overwhelmed, barely able to utter a mere 'Jesus, help me.' How wonderful to have a Christ-loving mom articulate such heartfelt, spot-on prayers—for nearly every circumstance! I so appreciate her faithfulness, her honesty, and her humor. This book should grace the waiting room of every doctor or therapist who serves special-needs families."

In *Special Grace*, you will find prayers for your frustration, grief, and above all, exhaustion. Prayers for when your child starts medication. Or undergoes a medication change. You'll find prayers for when your child creates a public scene. Prayers for bus drivers, for when people look at you funny; even prayers for your insurance company. Prayers for the celebration of the moment. And for growing up.

So, grab a cup of coffee and flip the page—by the last chapter, you may well discover how your life, so raw and visceral, can be beautiful. Messy, but beautiful. Gut wrenching, but wonderfully real. You'll discover a new friend in Elrena Evans, a Christ-loving mom who invites you to join her as she kneels at the throne on behalf of her family with special needs.

INTRODUCTION

*W*e are often *that* family.

The family people stare at for just a little too long, turning away quickly if we meet their gaze. The family children watch with wide eyes, perhaps waiting for a capable adult to intervene and restore order. We can sometimes pass for "typical"—if you ignore the fact that we have five kids, and three redheads, in our family of seven—but if you watch us a moment longer, or just catch us on a bad day, you'll see it. A child who hums and flaps his hands, oblivious to the outside world. A child who makes funny noises, or runs in circles. A child who can't control his fists. On a really bad day, you might see all of those things at the same time, and more.

But on a recent family trip to the Academy of Natural Sciences, for one brief moment in the café at lunchtime, we weren't *that* family. No one was crying because their sandwich wasn't perfectly sliced, or melting down because their food was too hot or too cold, or refusing to eat because the food was touching something else or was the wrong shape or the wrong shade or because someone heard a buzzing noise or one of the lights slightly flickered. No one was rocking in their seat or humming or fidgeting or making "atypical vocalizations." No one was upending a pepper shaker or sprinting across the room to push all the soda dispenser buttons.

In that one short moment—which lasted all of five minutes— another family passed by our table. The children were arguing, voices escalating, and the mother stopped, exasperated, and pointed at us.

"See those kids?" she asked. "See how they're all sitting at the table and eating their lunch so nicely? See how no one in their family is complaining or arguing?"

My children stopped eating, exchanged a few looks, and the older ones burst out laughing. We've been called out in public a lot; we're used to being *that* family. But I don't know if we've ever been that *other* family: the family that gets held up as the model. Because . . . that's not who we are.

• • •

This book is for all the parents of children with special needs, all the parents who "get it." Here are prayers for the exhaustion, frustration, and sheer joy of raising a child with disabilities. Here are prayers for laughter and heartache, for transitions, for bullies, for first days of therapy and last days of school. Here are words for the times we have none.

Our journeys are unique and I don't presume to say my journey has been anything like yours. But I pray that as you read this book, you will find glimpses of your own reflection, of the beauty and wonder of your story. I pray that you will find solace and comfort, and maybe a smile. I pray that these words may be yours when you need them, and that they may spur you on to create or find more words of your own as you travel this path with your child.

I've been an Episcopalian for decades, although not quite from the cradle, and I've taken a lot of inspiration for these prayers from the Book of Common Prayer. In addition to liturgies and directions for church services, the Book of Common Prayer contains many short-form prayers known as "collects." When I first started attending an Episcopal church, I read the word *collect* with the accent on the second syllable—but when I learned that the accent is in fact on the first syllable, and being a bit of a word nerd, I looked it up. The word *collect* comes from the Latin *collecta*, meaning "the gathering of the people together."

The collects are the prayers of the people who are gathered together. In other words, the body of Christ.

In keeping with this spirit, I've used the word *our* throughout the prayers in this book—our child, our family, our need. Raising a child with disabilities, whether we are single or partnered, often feels like a lonely, isolating journey. I've chosen to use the word *our* as a small reminder that we are not alone. There are other people out there who get it, who are also traveling this path. Maybe we haven't found them yet, but they are there—and my hope is that as you pray through these prayers, you will feel the prayers of those who pray them with you.

More than anything, I want you to know how amazing you are. Most of us didn't choose this path . . . and yet here we are, giving it our all. I think when God looks at us, he smiles.

I hope you will find the following prayers helpful to you on your journey.

1

BEGINNINGS

People were bringing little children to Jesus to have him touch them, but the disciples rebuked them. When Jesus saw this, he was indignant. He said to them, "Let the little children come to me, and do not hinder them, for the kingdom of God belongs to such as these. I tell you the truth, anyone who will not receive the kingdom of God like a little child will never enter it." And he took the children in his arms, put his hands on them and blessed them.

MARK 10:13-16

THE DIAGNOSIS

*W*hile trying to subdue one of my son's tantrums in the church hallway one Sunday, he knocked me to the ground. As I struggled to stand up without losing my hold on him, I turned away for a moment to try and explain his behavior to the growing crowd. As I did, he bit me, his teeth clamping into my skin until I had to wiggle his jaw to release them.

Weeks later, sitting in an empty classroom with my husband and the school psychologist for our first meeting, I looked at the sheaves of papers stacked high on the little desk beside me and thought, *Nothing in my life has prepared me for this moment.*

My son's first day at his new school was strictly choreographed: upon our arrival, five professionals separated him from me and walked him down the hall, name badges swinging from lanyards around their necks. It wasn't exactly the moment for a first-day-of-school photo opportunity, let alone any of the prettily worded prayers I'd seen on social media. Standing suddenly alone in the school office, I didn't have words.

• • •

The school psychologist who did my children's evaluations called me on the phone before our first official IEP meeting.

"I wanted to talk with you briefly before we meet," she said. She told me what a pleasure it was to work with my children, and what a remarkable family we have, before confirming that our middle son, then six, was indeed "different," in ways that would lead to a diagnosis and therapy and special education.

I balked. "Really? He has behavior problems, of course. Anyone can see that. And he's . . ." I paused before landing on my favorite go-to word for describing my children, ". . . quirky. He's quirky. But does that really mean he has 'special needs'?"

"I don't think you realize how atypical your son is," the school psychologist said gently, "because none of your children are typical. Your other children might just miss an actual diagnosis, but they clearly aren't what we would call typical."

I looked out the window to where my ten-year-old daughter was running in the backyard. She'd spent so much time running in the exact same circle that she'd worn down the grass to bare earth—we'd dubbed it "The Track." I watched her run, making odd little leaps into the air, her hands smacking against each other and occasionally reaching out to grasp things only she could see.

I looked over to my living room, where my eight-year-old son was also running, not in circles, but back and forth, back and forth. His fingers twisted into tumbling knots in front of his body as he ran, and when he stopped to jump, his upper torso knifed forward repeatedly. The tuneless hum filling the house was such a constant in my life I didn't even hear it anymore . . . it was just my son, running and humming, always running and humming.

And these were the children who were *not* receiving a diagnosis.

The psychologist had gone quiet, giving me a moment to think. "You're right," I finally said. "I think I don't realize how different my middle son is, because I'm mostly comparing him to his siblings."

His siblings had always been able to pass for "normal." Or normal-ish. Maybe not for the middle of the bell curve, but they could rein in their odd behaviors just enough to get by. They were quirky, to be sure, but they were never completely out of control. They were never violent.

But my middle son had flipped the script on that one, and I didn't know how best to parent him. How do you pray for a child who is violent? What are the words?

Thus began our journey into special education.

• • •

"This isn't my first rodeo," one of the many experts gathered around the table at our IEP meeting told me. "I've been working in special education for over a decade, and I have met a lot of special kids. But I have never seen anyone quite like your son."

I was exhausted from reading through stacks of papers, trying to understand my child in these new ways of charting and graphing, trying to process a world where learning the ABCs meant understanding Antecedents, Behaviors, and Consequences. I was still in the fog of alphabet soup acronyms ("Don't sign the NOREP until we figure out PCA or TSS!"), and my head was spinning as I watched the director of special education, the special education teacher, the behavioral specialist, the occupational therapist, the psychologist, and the "gifted" teacher all bringing the very best of their professional expertise to try to understand my son. While I jotted down question after question after question in the margins of my son's IEP, my husband drew increasingly complicated geometrical patterns all over his copy. We all cope in different ways.

At one point, I interrupted: "How do we know what part of my son's behavior is because he has special needs, and how much of it is just because . . . I don't know . . . he's being a little stinker?" I tried to clarify my question. "Did he really upend the desk because he didn't like the smell of the new markers? Or did he upend it just because he felt like it?"

The table grew quiet. My husband stopped doodling. The director of special education looked at me with a smile.

"*That* is the million-dollar question," she replied.

• • •

The lived reality of caring for my middle son's needs on top of the regular demands of parenting four other quirky children threatened to consume me. I started to worry more and more about our younger daughter, sandwiched in between an inherently needy infant and an older brother who now had a diagnosis. I watched and marked the trajectory of her behaviors, wondering, as always, where the line was between an outsized personality and a child with special needs.

Our younger daughter has always been fierce. As a toddler, when she wasn't pushing the furniture farther apart to see if she could still jump from one thing to another, she'd turn on the vacuum and chase her older siblings around with the hose. "Help! She's vacu-uming me again!" was a cry we heard multiple times a day. When my aunt asked me what she wanted for her birthday the year she turned two, I said, "World domination. But she would probably settle for an armored tank."

As other people's children seemed to mellow during the pre-school years, she only grew more intense. I brought up the question of her behavior with our family therapist: "What do I do with the fact that my kid *with* the diagnosis is currently doing better than the kid *without* the diagnosis? Does my daughter have special needs too?"

I paused, collecting my thoughts, and then continued. "How much of her behavior is inherently who she is, and how much of it is learned behavior from her older brother?"

"*That* is the million-dollar question," our therapist replied.

Apparently I ask a lot of million-dollar questions.

I imagined a possible future for my daughter, filled with more IEP meetings, more special education, more therapy. I wasn't sure how many more million-dollar questions I could handle.

• • •

Not long ago my middle son announced, out of the blue, "I like my new school. Because if you're a kid like me, and you need an aide, you can get one."

It stopped me short. But my heart said, *yes*. This I have words for. And a prayer. A prayer that we can pray together.

PRAYERS

For an Initial Diagnosis

O God, the Creator of everything, we are scared. We cannot see your plan right now, but we trust in your Word to guide us. Thank you that we live in a time when people are starting to understand difference, and thank you that through knowing this diagnosis, we are better equipped to meet the needs of your precious child. Walk with us, Lord, every step of this journey. In Jesus' Name, *Amen.*

For Decisions

God of all knowledge, this path you have put us on requires so many decisions. We often feel insufficient to the task. Surround us with people who give wise counsel, not foolish; who care for our needs, not their own advancement. In this decision we are facing now, God, be our guide. Show us your wisdom and give us your peace. *Amen.*

FOR TESTING

Lord, as we look to begin the testing process with [Name], we ask for mercy. We pray that this testing process be fair and accurate, and if a diagnosis is given, that it is fair and accurate too. Help us to know that a diagnosis is not the sum of [Name's] identity, but merely a tool that allows us access to further supports. Help us use these tools wisely to better understand and care for the child you have given us. Be with us during this difficult time. *Amen.*

A PRAYER FOR A PRENATAL DIAGNOSIS

Heavenly Father, we are scared. We are grieving. The future we are being asked to prepare for is not the future we had dreamed of. We haven't even met this child yet, but we know that you have. As you knit our baby's inmost being together in the secret of the womb, be with us. Surround us with your hope and comfort. In the Name of your precious Son, *Amen.*

IN TIMES OF FEAR

O God, who calmed the turbulent seas, your words speak peace to trembling hearts. The future is so uncertain, and right now we can't even figure out the present. Fear finds us in the night and steals our breath; fear robs us of our joy. Be with us in this place, Lord. Hold our fear as you hold our hearts. *Amen.*

WHEN FRUSTRATED

Unknot our minds, O God of Peace, in this moment of frustration. Clear our souls of distress. When we feel like we can't bear it one more second, remind us that you are the One who bears all things for us. Release us from annoyance and anger, and soothe us with your steadfast calm. *Amen.*

A Prayer for Exhaustion

Lord, you promise rest for the weary—and we are weary. We are bone-tired, in ways we didn't even know were possible. The day-to-day realities of caring for our child have left us bereft. Trying to prepare for a future we never imagined has left us feeling hopeless, and fear steals our sleep and floods our dreams. Help us to trust that you are not only our rock, Lord, but our place of safety too—a place of gentleness where we can fall, knowing that you will catch us and hold us always in your arms. *Amen.*

For Never-Ending Mountains of Paperwork

God of all things, we can't imagine how many trees were felled in service to the paperwork we are asked to complete for our child. We are tired of medical histories, social histories, educational histories. We are tired of trying to reduce the complexity and wonder of our child to lines on paper. And we are tired simply from filling out all these forms. Give us grace to persevere through a flawed and frustrating system. Meet our needs here, Lord, as we bring them ever to you. *Amen.*

When Faced with Uncertainty

God, we really like the illusion that we are in control, but this situation has punctured that illusion. Teach us that even when we can't see the next step, you are beside us. Teach us that we can trust you to stay with us. Teach us how to live with uncertainty. Give us wisdom and knowledge. As constant variables swirl around us, increase our assurance of your presence. In your changeless Name, *Amen.*

WHEN GOD DOESN'T HEAL

God of creation, you make all things beautiful in your perfect time. You are the God who walked the earth with us, bringing sight to the blind and sound to the deaf. We do not understand why you choose miraculous healing for some, but not for others. We remember your words to the blind man in the Gospel of John: "This happened so that the work of God might be displayed in his life." But sometimes we don't want to be your display, God. Sometimes we just want to be healed. Be with us in this pain. *Amen.*

FOR GRACE TO KEEP GOING

God of grace, be our grace.
God of the lost, find us.
God of grace, be our grace.
God of the broken, heal us.
God of grace, be our grace.
God of the suffering, succor us.
God of grace, be our grace.
Today, tomorrow, and evermore.
Amen.

2

FAMILY LIFE

Sing to God, sing praise to his name,
extol him who rides on the clouds—
his name is the Lord—
and rejoice before him.
A father to the fatherless, a defender of widows,
is God in his holy dwelling.
God sets the lonely in families,
he leads forth the prisoners with singing.

PSALM 68:4-6

THE DO-OVER

*T*he Saturday morning starts out innocuously enough. With my husband at praise band rehearsal at church, I tell the kids they can watch TV while I seize a rare opportunity to sleep in.

"But we made you breakfast in bed!" they call, which for reasons inexplicable to me they love to do.

"It's toast with butter and a little bit of cinnamon!" my twelve-year-old son enthuses.

"Where did you get the cinnamon?" I ask, slightly wary. The last I checked, we were out.

"Oh, it was spilled all over the counter," my seven-year-old daughter says.

"So we scraped it onto your toast," my nine-year-old son explains.

I take a bite. It is totally not cinnamon. It's cayenne pepper.

I eat the toast anyway. And I don't ask why cayenne pepper was spilled all over the counter. I don't need to ask. My nine-year-old—my middle son—was obviously cooking (or inventing, or experimenting) in the kitchen. Again.

When I come downstairs, I take a picture of the kitchen and send it to a friend—the open cupboards, the dishes piled on every counter, mysterious substances all over the floor, the aforementioned cayenne powder everywhere.

"This picture gives me anxiety," she writes back.

I often tell people that making and creating are ways my son makes sense of his world. For the most part it's a good thing. But sometimes things don't quite go according to plan, and he gets stuck in the inflexible parts of his brain. And then I have to clean up the mess.

Today, my son wants to make bread. Without a recipe. Or rather, with a recipe he has created himself. He explains his process to me as he pulls out flour, oil, baking soda, yeast, sugar, and blue food dye.

I listen resignedly. This is not going to go well, and I know it, but he is bound and determined to carry out his idea.

"Why don't we just make, ya know, actual bread?" I ask him. "We can even dye it blue."

"I want to make my *own* recipe," he replies.

"What is your backup plan if this doesn't work?" I ask him. The concept of a "backup plan" is a go-to for us, as it requires my son to think through an alternate plan before he gets stuck on the first one. Then, if something doesn't work out the way he thinks it will, we've already laid the foundation for Plan B.

But he is, as usual, resistant to the backup plan.

"Nothing will go wrong," he says, dumping flour into a bowl. "I've thought it all out."

"But just in case," I say. "Humor me."

"But it *won't!*" His voice ratchets up a notch. "I've thought it all out!"

I survey the mess surrounding me, the scowl on his face. Nope, this is not going to go well.

An hour later, every surface in the entire kitchen is covered in flour or oil or both, and my son is donning oven mitts before pulling a smoking Pyrex pan of paste from the toaster oven. I ask my oldest two children to take the youngest two outside before I venture into his workspace.

"Congratulations," I want to tell him. "You've trashed the entire kitchen and made warm, blue glue."

But I can't tell him that. And he can't let go of the idea of his creation.

"Why didn't this *work?*" he says. "I thought it all out!"

He drops the pan in the sink with a clatter and reaches for the flour.

"I'm going to make it again," he declares.

"Honey," I tell him. "I think if we're going to make more bread we really need to follow a recipe."

"But I want to make my *own* recipe," he says again. "I've thought it all out! It will *work!*" He's getting more and more frustrated, and I'm facing a Saturday spent navigating escalating tantrums in the kitchen among spilled flour and oil.

"But this isn't working," I tell him firmly. "We need a Do-Over."

• • •

When my son was younger, before his diagnosis, our days were marked by moments of his frenetic, extreme, uncontrollable energy.

That was before we filled our house with exercise balls and a balance beam and a rocker board and a Spooner board and a chin-up bar and a zoom ball and a Bosu ball and more. At one point, we owned so many gadgets to assist my son with his need for "big movements," as we called them, that when I tore a ligament in my ankle and wound up in physical therapy, half the gadgets in the physical therapy gym seemed like old friends.

"Oh, I have that at home," I would say to my therapist, as she brought out stretch bands, weights, and slant boards. When I told her we had our own balance beam, she asked, "Is there anything here you *don't* have?"

I looked around. "We don't have the harness that hangs from a track on the ceiling," I said. "But other than that? Yeah, we pretty much have all your stuff."

Because we needed all the stuff to help my son regulate his body.

It was on one such extreme-energy day, when my son was five, that the concept of the Do-Over was born.

It had been a rough day. My son lost all control over himself and flew through the house, dumping anything and everything he could get his hands on. First, he squirted out an entire bottle of dish soap on the floor in the kitchen. I got him temporarily settled down in his room with his LEGO bricks and started to clean it up—but he abandoned the LEGO bricks, ran to the fireplace, took the small shovel from the fireplace tools, and starting heaving shovelfuls of ash all over the living room. After I stopped him and settled him down with a snack, I started vacuuming up the ashes—but he ran into the kitchen and took all of the spice jars out of the cupboard and dumped them on the kitchen counter. While I was cleaning up spices, having resorted to turning on the TV for him, he ran upstairs and squirted out two different bottles of shaving cream all over the bathroom sink, the walls, the mirror, the toilet, the floor. While cleaning up the shaving cream, I saw him running up the stairs with a sippy cup of water . . . minus the valve, pouring water all the way up the stairs.

And I lost it.

"What are you *doing*?" I yelled at a volume that could rival my three-year-old daughter's. "Can't you just stop it? *Stop* it! Just *stop!*" I grabbed the cup out of his hand and righted it.

My son startled, then looked at the cup. "I didn't know it was upside-down," he said.

And he started to cry. Clearly, whatever had been driving him to wreak havoc on the house wasn't also propelling him now to dump water. The spilled water had been an accident.

"Oh buddy, I'm so sorry," I said, sinking down on my knees and putting my hands on his shoulders. He shrugged me off. "I thought you were dumping the water on purpose. I'm so sorry."

I think fast. "Can we have a rewind and we'll try again?"

"A rewind?" my son asked.

"A rewind!" I said, handing the cup back to him. "Turn the cup back upside-down. Then see if you can walk backward down the stairs."

He stared at me, but then took the cup, and began walking backward down the stairs. As he walked, the cup leaking all over the floor, I made "rewind" noises, as if I was talking backward. Then I called for him to come up the stairs again, still with the cup upside-down.

"Okay, take two!" I said. He rounded the corner and came up the stairs, the cup leaking out the last of its contents on the floor.

"Hey, buddy!" I called. "I don't know if you noticed, but your cup is upside-down. Wanna turn it right-side up?" He looked at me, flipped his cup over, and grinned.

"Much better," I said. "Thanks for giving me a Do-Over." I reached out and ruffled his hair. "I love you lots and lots."

He kicked me in the shin, unsurprisingly. But then he said, "I love you too."

• • •

Standing in the kitchen surrounded by bowls overflowing with blue ingredients and pots of leaking goo, I look at my son. I can feel the anger and frustration radiating off him. He planned this all out in his head. Why didn't it work?

My seven-year-old appears in the kitchen. "I want homemade mac and cheese!" she yells.

"Could you please restate your demand in the form of a polite question?" I respond. This is a line of my husband's, and I love it. But she does not restate her demand in the form of a polite question.

"MAC! AND! CHEESE!"

My son scowls. "Get her out of the kitchen." His fingers tighten into fists inside the oven mitts.

I turn and put my hands on my daughter's shoulders. "Sweetie, can you just go back outside with your siblings? Or do you want to watch another show, and then we'll figure out food?" As always, I feel guilty that the TV is coparenting my other kids while I try to help my son, floundering in his own frustration and inability to change his mind, to restart—to Do-Over.

"Do you think we could just try a Do-Over?" I ask again. "Take the pan out of the sink. Walk backward. I can't unmake the bread, because that involves chemical reactions . . . but we can start again from scratch."

I pause. "And you can make your own recipe. All I ask is that you wait until Daddy comes home, because he can help you with the science behind bread making. He can talk you through the chemical reactions of baking powder, and tell you all about how yeast is a fungus, and teach you the different proteins in gluten and why they matter."

My son looks at me. I can see I have his interest. I keep talking, fast.

"Do you know the scientific name for yeast?" I ask him.

"No," he says.

"Me either. But I bet you anything Daddy does. And he can tell you. And once you understand the science, you can make your own recipe. Your very own recipe for blue bread."

My son pauses. The temptation of learning something that I don't know is a big one. He slides the oven mitt off his hand.

"Do-Over?" I ask.

"Okay," he finally says. "Can I play Minecraft until Daddy comes home?"

"Absolutely," I say. He runs into the playroom. And I send my husband a quick text: *Rough morning. Baking blue bread when you get home. Possibly homemade mac & cheese? Be prepared.*

PRAYERS

FOR HOME LIFE

O God who orders our common life and holds our days, bless our home. Bless its inhabitants, bless our coming and going, bless our waking and sleeping. Give us abundant laughter and bountiful joy. Knit our hearts together in such reciprocal love and affection that we may see glimpses of you in all of our relationships. Thank you for our child [Name]. Thank you for the gift of [his/her] life, and thank you that you've chosen us to share in that life too. In the Name of your Son, *Amen.*

FOR PARENTS

O God, who calls ordinary people to do extraordinary things, remind us that in our ordinariness we were fashioned by the One who spun galaxies from dust. Assure us that the One who holds the universe is holding us. Bless us as we care for this child of yours, [Name]. Give us your love to be our love. Give us your strength to be our strength. Give us your joy to be our joy. Make us always mindful that this child is your precious creation, and help us always to see [him/her] with your eyes. *Amen.*

FOR SIBLINGS

O God, you gave us the gift of childhood, and placed us in families to learn about your love. Thank you for our child [Sibling's Name]. We know this child's life is fundamentally shaped by the sibling(s) [he/she] has been given, and we're conscious of the ways that life is different. Forgive us, Lord, for interpreting that difference as deficiency. Forgive us for blaming ourselves for failing to achieve what we perceive as "normal." Assure us that You are always enough. Help us to see the ways our child's life has been enriched for growing up so close to [his/her] sibling(s). *Amen.*

FOR EXTENDED FAMILY

God of community and connection, our extended families, as you know, can be tricky. Thank you for the people you have placed in our lives who understand our child; give us unmeasured grace with those who don't. Help us to see goodwill even in the bumbling and the missteps. Soften all of our hearts, Lord. Give us moments and memories of joy. *Amen.*

FOR GRACE IN HOUSEWORK

Dear God, we can't keep up. Too often this household feels like a juggling match teetering on the edge of collapse, with balls and pins and spinning plates flying everywhere and clonking us on the head. We can't do this. Help us prioritize what's important, Lord. Help us to know what, and when, to let go. Help us to believe that the God of lilies and sparrows cares whether or not we have clean underwear. And help us trust that your plans for our lives transcend the dishes and laundry. *Amen.*

For Mealtime

O God who created a bounty of foods to nourish and sustain us, you called that provision good. And you create friendship and fellowship through the ritual of eating together. But sometimes mealtime seems so fraught. Juggling our child's needs and our own desires and what seems like an infinite list of demands seems too much, when all we want is to feed and be fed. Be with us as we break our bread, Lord . . . and our vegetables and fruits and meats. Remind us that you are the Bread of Life, you are the One who sustains us. *Amen.*

For Understanding Employers

God of provision, thank you for the gift of work. Be with our employer(s), Lord. Give them understanding, compassion, and tolerance; help them to be lenient when needed. As we navigate this tricky territory of competing work lives and home lives, all while caring for our child, help our employer(s) to be a blessing, not a burden. Help us not to get fired. And help us not to hide at work, when it's easier than what awaits us at home. In your holy Name, *Amen.*

A Prayer for the Morning

O God, be with us this day as we rise to do your work. When our feet feel too heavy to drag out of bed, give us the lightness of grace. When the "do" list stretches ever longer than the "done" list, remind us that you are in control. When the needs of our child threaten to topple us, shore us up with your strength. Helps us to give this day to you, Lord. It was always yours anyway. *Amen.*

A Prayer for the Middle of the Night

Lord, you tell us that even the darkness is light to you. Be our light in the darkness tonight. As the world around us sleeps, comfort us in our wakefulness. Calm our racing hearts and frantic minds. Help us to surrender our burdens to you so that in turn we may surrender ourselves to sweet sleep. Wake us in the morning refreshed in your love. *Amen.*

For Comfort

God of the hurting, we cry to you.
Comfort us.
God of the weeping, we cry to you.
Comfort us.
God of the broken, we cry to you.
Comfort us.
Be with us now in this moment of our pain.
Infuse our spirits with your solace.
Be our God of comfort.
Amen.

A Prayer Before a Home Visit

God, we know this person is coming today to help us, but sometimes we feel like we're on trial. Is it not enough that we have to be clean, fed, and presentable? Now our house has to look good too?

This is unfair. We know we're good parents regardless of the crayon on the wall, the sneakers in the freezer, or the size of the laundry pile. But we still feel judged. Help our visitor to understand that the state of the house is not indicative of the level of care we give our child, but is *because* of the care we give our child. Calm our nerves. Be with us today. *Amen.*

FOR RESPITE CARE

God, we thank you for respite care and respite care providers. Be with [Name and Name] as they care for our child. In the moments when they feel overwhelmed, bring your peace. In the moments when they feel exhausted, bring your rest. In every moment of their days, bring your joy. Help them care for our child in our absence, and bless them in their work. *Amen.*

FOR A SETBACK

Heavenly Father, we don't understand why this setback is happening. The progress we were making seems to be coming to an end, and we are frustrated, angry, and scared. We do not know where to turn, and it is hard when we cannot see your perfect purpose in our lives. Give us grace to weather this change, to know how to move forward, and to accept this time of setback. Show us your abundant mercy wherever we find ourselves. In your holy Name, *Amen.*

A PRAYER FOR A LOVED ONE WHO IS OUT OF CONTROL

God who brought order out of chaos, be with our beloved [Name]. God who hung the sun in the sky, be the light in [Name's] darkness. God who calmed the seas, calm [Name's] soul. God who sent your angels to say "Do not be afraid," minister to [Name's] fear as only you can. Comfort, heal, and surround us, Lord. In your most precious and holy Name, *Amen.*

A Prayer for a Meltdown

Break through this moment, Lord, and be with us. Where we need comfort, be our consolation. Where we need safety, be our protection. Where we need resolution, be our peace. Loose the chokehold of fear and flood us with your quietude. Surround us with your unfathomable light. *Amen.*

Another Prayer for a Meltdown

God of grace,
Comfort us.
Protect us.
Be our peace and light.
Amen.

A Prayer for Strength

God, it is only in your strength that we find our strength. Breathe your strength into us as you once formed the world with your breath. Renew our bodies. Comfort our minds. Show us the moments of rest and respite you have tucked into our everyday lives, and let every one of those moments point us back to you. *Amen.*

When We Feel Like We're Failing

Dear God, sometimes we feel like we're failing at everything and we just can't keep up. When doubt screams in our ears, whisper the truth: that in your perfect grace, we are enough. Help us turn our eyes away from the mountain of evidence we've amassed that says we're not doing a good enough job; help us remember all that we give to love and raise this child. Remind us that this hard work is the work you have called us to do, and that you are always with us. When we feel like we are falling, Lord, catch us. Promise us that you won't let us fall too far. In your Name, *Amen.*

A Prayer for When Everything Seems to Be Going Wrong

Dear God, we are frustrated, overwhelmed, and confused. Our thoughts feel murky and we don't know what to do. Every step we take seems to lead in the wrong direction. We have been very tired for a very, very long time. Be with us as we muddle through this day. Remind us that, at the end, there is you. *Amen.*

Another Prayer for When Everything Seems to Be Going Wrong

Dear God, what is with this day? We are trying to believe that you are not capricious and cruel, but it's hard, Lord, when we feel like we can't catch a break. Be an oasis of calm in our chaos. Bring your order into our shambles. Breathe on us, until in every breath we feel your presence. And also, can you fix this mess? *Amen.*

One More Prayer for When Everything Seems to Be Going Wrong

Dear God, we cannot even today. In Jesus' Name, *Amen.*

WHEN WE WANT TO QUIT

Heavenly Father, be the anchor of hope when we want to give up, and the ground beneath our feet when we lose faith. Give us wisdom to see when the answer is to keep going, and when the answer is to reach out to others for help. Bring into our lives those people who can help us, and give us the grace to accept their help, even when we don't want to. In your Name, *Amen.*

3

SCHOOL

You will keep in perfect peace
him whose mind is steadfast,
because he trusts in you.
Trust in the Lord forever,
for the Lord, the Lord, is the Rock eternal.

THE SUBSTITUTE
TEACHER PROBLEM

*T*he doors swing open on the elementary school bus, and neighborhood children come tumbling out. I hold my preschooler's hand as I give my seven-year-old daughter a welcome-home hug, then look up for a moment of brief eye contact with the bus driver. My nine-year-old, my middle son, didn't get off the bus.

"Did he get on?" I mouth over my daughter's head.

The bus driver nods, eyes on the rearview mirror where she can see the back of the bus. "He's coming," she says, and raises her eyebrows at me.

No further explanation is needed. After years of shorthand communication with our bus driver—not to mention nine years of raising my son—I know to brace for impact. My son explodes from the bus like a thunderclap.

"I'm so happy to see you!" I say as he scowls. We've learned over the years never to ask him a question as he's getting off the bus and reintegrating into family life, so all I say, every day, is that I'm happy to see him. A simple "How are you?" or "How was your day?" is enough to make him unravel.

Today, he doesn't need any help with the unraveling. He's already most of the way there.

"We had a *sub*," he snarls as he flings his backpack at me and bolts toward the house. And I understand. His routine has been disrupted, and now our entire family will feel the effects for the rest of the day—maybe longer.

• • •

When my son was in first grade, he decided to solve the substitute teacher problem himself. His special education teacher relayed the story to me at one of our IEP meetings.

"He says he's going to code a robot," she said. "He told me if we can replace all substitute teachers with robots, we can program them so that all outputs match known inputs, and thus eliminate any break in routine."

"At least he's not trying his hand at cloning," I said. "Yet."

Disruptions in routine are hard for my son. Social cues are hard. Relating to people is hard. Anything that doesn't go the way he anticipated is hard. Obviously, the most logical answer is robots. In a world without tricky and unpredictable humans, he would probably do much better. Inputs and outputs. Black and white. No confusing things like decorative pillows ("Why have pillows that you don't use for sleeping?") or women wearing makeup ("Why are they putting that stuff on their face? What are they trying to hide?").

• • •

As feared, the effects of the substitute teacher reverberate through the afternoon and into the night. My son runs through the house, crashing into things, making "atypical vocalizations" at full volume. "Can't you be *quiet*?!" my twelve-year-old asks. "I'm trying to do my vocab!"

"No, he can't," my fourteen-year-old replies. "He can't, or he *won't*," she adds darkly.

I ferry my daughters to and from ballet class, read to my preschooler, and help my oldest son with his vocabulary. As my husband is making dinner, I find a moment of peace with my middle son, curled up with him on the couch wrapped in one of his fuzzy blankets.

"Substitute teachers are hard," I say, as he rams his head against my shoulder.

"This one was *the worst*," he growls.

"I'm sorry you felt that way," I say.

"But he's right!" my seven-year-old interjects. "A lot of the time he just *says* the sub was bad. But I *know* this sub. She is the *literal actual* worst." My daughter pauses for dramatic effect. "She is *sooo* bad."

I sigh. It's going to be a long night.

By morning, the "substitute effect" has snowballed. Because he was thrown off his routine, my son didn't do his homework. Because he was angry about the homework, he refused to eat breakfast. My four other children are orbiting around me as I try to coax him to eat and help him finish his homework. His class is having a pajama party today, and I know he won't be allowed to participate unless his homework is finished.

"Can someone get me some spicy frappuccinos?" my preschooler asks. (He means pepperoncini—pickled chili peppers—which he likes to eat in the morning alongside his breakfast cereal. What can I say? Our family is a little quirky.)

"Just write one more sentence," I plead with my middle son, sliding a bite of bagel into his mouth as he yells.

"Can someone get me some spicy frappuccinos?" my preschooler repeats.

"Mom, did you proofread my essay?" my older daughter asks.

"I can't find my vocab book!" my oldest son yells.

"Did you sign my planner?" my seven-year-old calls.

"AND WILL SOMEONE GET ME SOME SPICY FRAPPUCCINOS?"

In the middle of it all—my son. He's sitting at the table, in his pajamas, clutching a teddy bear and crying. All he wants to do is go to school and have a normal day, followed by a pajama party. But the homework. But the breakfast. But the sub. But the millions of tiny details he can't control or navigate, the world that is just too complicated for him to process.

I want to press pause, give him the time and space he needs to figure things out. But the bus is coming in single-digit minutes. I think of all the children, like my son, struggling to fit into a world that wasn't designed for them. One friend's nonverbal son who can't tell her what went wrong with his day. Another friend's daughter who received the wrong-sized headpiece for her cochlear implants. One other friend's son who nearly died when food was cross-contaminated with one of his allergens.

I think of all the children, the ones I know and the millions I don't, whose families need just a little extra grace.

My son snaps me out of my reverie as he crams the last of his bagel in his mouth and stuffs his homework into his bag. Later, I'll receive a note from his special education teacher that he was able to complete his assignment at school, before the pajama party, and I'll get a picture of him smiling and happy, clutching his bear on a blanket in his classroom.

But I don't know that now. All I can do in this moment is find his shoes and my oldest son's vocab book and sign my daughter's planner and serve up one more spicy frappuccino as we race to the bus. *I want to give you the world*, I think, as my children tumble toward the opening bus doors. But more than that, *I want to give you a world where you fit in.*

My son adjusts his backpack and squeezes his teddy bear. "DEAR GOD," he says, as he climbs the bus steps, "PLEASE do not let us have a sub again today."

Amen, I say to his retreating back. *Amen and amen.*

PRAYERS

At the Start of the School Year

God of all knowledge, we come to you at the start of a new school year for our child [Name]. We don't know what this year will bring. We are excited, anxious, aspiring, and worried, and right now our feelings are all jumbled up inside us. Thank you for the gift of education, and for the minds and hearts that will touch ours this year. Give us strength in our challenges, and joy in our successes, and let us always be mindful that you are with us. *Amen.*

A Blessing for the First Day of School

May there be smooth mornings, unhampered by overexcitement or dread, and no lost socks, devices, school supplies, or tempers.

May everyone eat breakfast.

May your car or bus ride be worry-free, your classrooms bright and welcoming, and your teachers kind and understanding.

May the unfamiliar faces around you hide true friends you will soon discover.

May you have the ability to tune out when you need to, and tune in when you need to, and not be overwhelmed.

May lockers open with ease, classroom locations be findable, and transitions be simple.

May you have someone to sit with at lunch.

May you have strength to make it through the whole day; may your afternoon be as bright as your morning.

May your trip home be uneventful.

May you rally when you see your family, so that your coming home will be a time of joy and not stress.

May God be with you every step of the day.

FOR RIDING THE BUS

Heavenly Father, we are terrified of the bus. In this liminal space between home and school, protect our child. Protect [him/her] from injury, both physical and emotional, and make this lumbering yellow machine an unexpected haven of safety and respite. Thank you that we have this resource available to us, and help us never to take it for granted. In your Name, *Amen.*

FOR BUS DRIVERS

Lord God, thank you for our bus driver. Thank you for this person who transports our child safely to and from school every day. Give our bus driver focus, Lord, and limitless patience. As [he/she] juggles both the demands of the road and the needs of the children on board, give [him/her] your supernatural peace. In Jesus' Name, *Amen.*

FOR TEACHERS

God who first taught us to love you, be with our teachers this year. Give them the knowledge they need to teach us, and the love they need to understand us. Bless their willingness to think outside the box, Lord, for they will surely need to this year. Help them see our child for who our child is: a spark of your light in this world. In your Name, *Amen.*

FOR SPECIAL EDUCATION TEACHERS

Dear God, thank you for special education teachers. Thank you for giving them the passion to serve, the dedication to learn, and the sheer stick-with-it-ness to persevere. As they grow to know our child, bless their relationship. May they build mutual trust so that growth and learning may occur. And bless them with rest, Lord. We both know they're going to need it. *Amen.*

FOR AN AIDE

Dear Lord, we thank you for our child's aide, [Name]. Thank you for the gifts you have given [him/her], and for the ability to come alongside our child and be your hands and feet throughout the day. Bless those hands and feet, Lord. Bless the knowledge, skill, and dedication which in turn blesses not only our child, but our entire family. Bless [Name's] willingness to serve, and foster the relationship with our child so that, in an environment of mutual respect and affection, trust may flourish. Thank you, Lord. *Amen.*

FOR A SUBSTITUTE TEACHER

Dear God, well, you know what's coming and I know what's coming, but this dear teacher has no idea. Give our substitute teacher a good day, Lord. Make the morning so perfect and unhampered that [he/she] arrives at school in the very best possible mood, overflowing with a grace that will spill out all over our child. Give [him/her] strength throughout the day, and rest and respite tonight, Lord—we know it will be needed. Thank you for all substitute teachers everywhere, who daily walk into classrooms of unknown children and daily give their very best. Bless them abundantly. Especially when those classrooms include our child. In Jesus' Name, *Amen.*

FOR A DIFFICULT TEACHER/AIDE

God of creativity and complexity, you made us all so different. And in that difference there is beauty—but sometimes, there is also friction. Some people just don't "click," Lord, and right now we have a [teacher/aide] who doesn't click with our child. Give us your grace. Help us to know when to speak up and advocate for our child, and when to just grit our teeth and thank you that this relationship is only (hopefully!) for one year. Through it all, Lord, protect our child. Be with [him/her] always. In your holy Name, *Amen.*

FOR BULLYING

God, our hearts break when we see the pain and devastation brought about by bullying. Show us opportunities to speak up when the situation warrants, and grant us the power to hold our tongues when needed. Protect and shield us from the poisoned darts of cruel words and actions. Give us, Lord, in your incomparable grace, the ability to see even bullies as you see them: priceless children of God. Bring about a resolution to this situation, Lord, as only you can. In the Name of the One who loves us all, *Amen.*

FOR BULLIES

God of all children, we see the pain in this child who is bullying ours. Even if we don't know what's causing it, be with this child in that pain. Help us to remember that we do not know everything about this child's home life, school life, or innermost thoughts. Help us to remember that all of your children deserve to be cherished and dearly loved. Give us abundant compassion for children who do not know that love. Make us instruments of your peace. *Amen.*

FOR A FIELD TRIP

Dear God, we thank you for this opportunity for our child [Name] to go on a field trip. We're excited, Lord! We're also a little scared. Help us focus on the positives, instead of all the things that could go wrong. All the many, many things that could go wrong. Help, Lord. Thank you for giving us people who make our participation possible; thank you for all those who will attend to our needs on this trip. Help us to have a good day, Lord. And bring us safely back home tonight. *Amen.*

BEFORE AN IEP MEETING

Lord, bless all those who will assemble in this meeting today to determine an educational plan for our child. Give us clear minds, coherent goals, and the ability to work with one another in the best interest of our child. Thank you for special education and accommodation and all the abundance of resources you have provided for our child. Thank you for this team. In your Name, *Amen.*

Before Another IEP Meeting

Dear God, you know. We've done this before. Help us to remember, when we are frustrated, that we all want what's best for our child, even when we disagree on what that "best" is. Help us to communicate clearly, advocate wisely, and above all, entrust our child into the loving arms of the One who loves [him/her] even more than we do. Give us your peace, Lord. *Amen.*

Before Yet Another IEP Meeting

Dear God, we're done. We are frustrated that the plans we thought would work for our child have not; we're angry at our inability to find solutions. We just want to do what's best for our child, Lord, and we're trying. But right now we just want to quit. Give us strength, Lord. Bless the team. Foster in us all a sense of cohesiveness that, through our combined efforts, we might all work in the best interest of your child. Be with us, Lord. And please let this be the last revision, at least for a while? *Amen.*

4

PUBLIC LIFE

Some men came carrying a paralytic on a mat and tried to take him into the house to lay him before Jesus. When they could not find a way to do this because of the crowd, they went up on the roof and lowered him on his mat through the tiles into the middle of the crowd, right in front of Jesus. When Jesus saw their faith, he said, "Friend, your sins are forgiven."

LUKE 5:18-20

SUNDAY MORNING
MINECRAFT

Sunday morning, nine o'clock. As the first notes of the prelude swell out from the church organ, my husband is sitting in the sanctuary with the praise band. My fourteen-year-old is in her acolyte robe, ready to process with the clergy and choir. My twelve-year-old is sitting in the tech booth, where he's working the church camera for the service. My seven-year-old daughter and four-year-old son are in Sunday school. And my nine-year-old is sitting in the church library, with me, where he will spend Sunday morning playing Minecraft.

"Do you want to try going into the sanctuary for Communion today?" I ask him.

"No," he says.

Church is a particularly challenging environment for my son. And the older he's gotten, the more of a challenge it has become. A few weeks ago, as he was melting down in the fellowship hall, a well-meaning parishioner looked at me and smiled.

"There's one in every family!" she said, as she stirred her coffee and walked away.

I looked at her retreating back and thought, *Actually? Statistically? There's not. There isn't a child like my son in every family.*

I know what she means—there's a "difficult" child in every family—but my son isn't difficult. My son has special needs. It's different.

I email a good friend, also the mother of a child with special needs, to vent about church. She suggests we just take some time off—stop trying, stop going for a while. The exhaustion of just trying to get five kids out the door, let alone help my son navigate all the expectations of Sunday morning, is doing me in, and she knows it. She hears about it every week.

I write her back. "I think I would do better at church if people didn't smile at me. I see all these people, and they smile, and it's like they're saying, 'Isn't it so great to be here?' And I want to say 'Do you see me? Really, truly *see* me? Because I am dying over here. Please don't make me feel invisible.'"

• • •

When my son was a toddler, he loved going to church. What's not to love? Playground time, goldfish crackers in Sunday school, donuts in the fellowship hall after the service. Sure, he had some trouble controlling his feet and his fists—but many two- and three-year-olds do. He could still linger close enough to the middle of the bell curve to avoid setting off alarms.

In our church atrium stands a giant statue of the Good Samaritan helping the injured man on the side of the road. Slightly larger-than-life, featureless figures, the arms of the Samaritan bend around to gently help the injured man as he lifts his head. Mostly, it serves as an indoor playground for kids to climb and swing on. My son was no exception: climbing on the head of the Good Samaritan might have been his favorite thing about church.

One day, my oldest son, then four, started quizzing him on the parable as he swung and climbed.

"What did this man do?" my oldest son asked, patting the head of the injured man.

"Crying!" my toddler son called out, moving to pat the man's head as well.

"And what did this other man do?"

"Holdin' hands! Help . . . walk! *Care* for him!"

Every time I pass the statue I can picture my tiny blond son, sitting there in his puffy blue winter coat, patting the man's head: "*Care* for him!"

Things began to shift around the time my son was in kindergarten. Every Sunday, the children's ministries director would appear at the end of our pew, holding my son by the hand. "He hit one of the teachers," she would tell me. "He threw a chair. He scratched another child." This weekly appearance quickly became our new routine, with my son being brought into the sanctuary earlier and earlier each week. Eventually, we couldn't make it past the opening hymn without my son appearing at our pew. As other children were learning to sit in a circle for Bible stories, sing simple songs, and memorize verses, my son was starting to look more and more like an outlier.

We tried to make it work.

We tried sticker charts, marble jars, rewards, and consequences. We took away screen time. We read more Scripture. Sunday mornings before church I would carefully trim my son's fingernails (we made time to do this, every Sunday morning, in a house with five kids under the age of ten), and I would talk to him about not scratching, not hitting, keeping his hands to himself.

He couldn't do it.

A parishioner who works with children who have special needs volunteered to be his "buddy." We hired a professional aide. The church added sensory items to the classroom and held training sessions for the team of volunteer teachers. But nothing seemed to work.

Our church brought in a representative from Joni & Friends to talk about disability ministries. And that was when I had my epiphany.

"What do you currently do on Sunday mornings?" she asked me.

"We sit in the church library while he plays Minecraft," I answered, feeling my face redden with shame.

"The Holy Spirit is present in the church library too," she said. "God can meet your son there as easily as in the sanctuary."

So on Sunday mornings, we sit in the library and play Minecraft. With the door open I can hear the strains of music floating up from the sanctuary below; sometimes I drift out into the hallway to listen. The praise band for the later service practices in an adjoining room during the sermon, and I can hear them too. More music and less preaching is absolutely fine by me.

But Communion pulls at my heart. I want my family all in church together, kneeling at the altar rail, receiving Communion every week. I think about the Nicene Creed, our profession of faith that we recite each Sunday: "We believe in the communion of saints, the forgiveness of sins, the resurrection of the body, and the life everlasting."

Sitting in the church library, watching my son play Minecraft, I am grieving the loss of the communion of saints.

"Do you want to try going in for Communion today?" I ask.

"No."

"Will you be okay here by yourself for a few minutes if I go down to the sanctuary?"

He shrugs. I decide to take that as an affirmative, and go downstairs alone—cutting the line so I can join my husband and other children as they approach the Communion rail.

But I still hear echoes of my son's toddler voice as I walk through the church: "*Care* for him!"

Is that what I am doing? Letting him play Minecraft in the library? And if there were another, better, way to care for him . . . would I know?

PRAYERS

A Prayer Before Going Out

Dear God, sometimes we miss the days when "going out" meant grabbing our shoes and keys and waltzing out the door. Often we look at all the barriers to leaving the house with our child, and it just doesn't seem worth it. Be with us today, Lord. Bless our efforts, bless those with whom we come in contact. Bless our going out and our coming home, that we may spend our entire day, no matter where we find ourselves, cocooned in your love. *Amen.*

A Prayer for Being "That Family"

Dear God, can't we just catch a break? We see the looks, the sidelong sneers, the covert and not-so-covert judgments aimed our way. When we want to either die of embarrassment or put someone else in their place, help us to remember that we don't fully know these people or their contexts any better than they know us or ours. Help us to be the bigger person, God. (Actually: scratch that. We are sick of being the bigger person. Please make someone else take a turn for once.) *Amen.*

FOR DISCRIMINATION

God of the broken, we know your heart breaks when you see the hatred your children unleash on each other. Because we are uniquely positioned to experience that hatred, we see the effects of discrimination so sharply. We cry out, Lord, against those who judge us for being different. You made us different, Lord, and even though we do not always understand why, we know that you see us as perfect and holy and worthy of love, reflecting your beauty in the world. Help others to see us that way too. *Amen.*

FOR ACCOMMODATION

Lord, be with us as we prepare to make a request for accommodation. Help us to articulate our requests wisely and with sensitivity, and give those to whom we address our needs compassion and understanding. Help us all work together in the best interest of our child, and meet our needs as only you can. In your Name, *Amen.*

A PRAYER FOR A PUBLIC SCENE

Dear God, we are so embarrassed. We would like to say, "on behalf of our child," but the truth is, we're embarrassed for ourselves. And we're angry at a world that isn't designed for families like ours. We are frustrated, grieving, and above all, exhausted. Thank you that you are with us even when you feel so far away. Thank you that the events of today were merely a moment in time and not an eternity. Help us not to mentally calculate exactly how many more of these moments we might get to experience. And help us remember that you love our child even more than we do and that you are always with us, enfolding us in your arms. *Amen.*

FOR MOBILE THERAPISTS

Lord, we thank you for [Name], and for [his/her] work with our child in this setting. Thank you for the years of hard work and education on behalf of children like our own. Bless them in their endeavors here, that they may be fruitful, and that through the development of a mutual relationship our child might flourish. In your Name, *Amen.*

FOR FRIENDS

Dear God, thank you for our friends. Thank you for the people you've brought into our lives—to walk beside us, to carry our burdens, to love us. Thank you for the care that our friends have for our child. Thank you for the myriad ways our friends are brightly shining lights that point the way to you. *Amen.*

FOR THE CHURCH

Dear God, when you chose to establish your church as a collection of your people, you knew that the church would be a place both of healing and of hurt. Because we're people, after all. Thank you for all the ways the church has been a place of solace, friendship, and comfort. Mend our hearts in all the places where the church has hurt us and made us feel alienated, ostracized, and scarred. Be with us, Lord, as we strive to live in unity with all your children, even when it's difficult. Especially when it's difficult. *Amen.*

WHEN PEOPLE SPIRITUALIZE DISABILITY

Maker of the universe, we are in awe of your creation. From the spiraling arms of the galaxies to the intricate whorls of the inner ear, this world—and the people within it—are fearfully and wonderfully made. We don't understand disability, Lord. We don't understand why you made our child different. If it was to show your glory, that seems mean. And we can't stand the comments from people who seek to prop their theology on our experience. Help us to embrace even what we can't understand, Lord. Help us to make space for uncertainty. Help us, always, to trust you. *Amen.*

WHEN PEOPLE LOOK AT US FUNNY

Dear God, sometimes we cannot even step outside without someone staring at us. This seems monstrously unfair and we hate it. Forgive us for always seeing cruelty in a gaze that may simply be curious . . . and change their stares as you change their hearts. Change ours too. *Amen.*

ANOTHER PRAYER FOR WHEN PEOPLE LOOK AT US FUNNY

Dear God, we saw that. Help us to unsee that. Or at the very least, to forgive. Give us your eyes, Lord. And your grace. *Amen.*

WHEN PEOPLE SAY REALLY DUMB THINGS

God, when you gave us the gift of language, with that came the ability to say really dumb things. Give us grace to bite back our snarky comments, our quick retorts, the things we really want to say to the know-it-alls who think they would surely be doing much better in our shoes. Help us to remember that they only know what they know. Give us eyes to see them as you see them. Stall our tongues and, if needed, our feet and our fists. *Amen.*

WHEN PEOPLE ARE "INSPIRED" BY US

Heavenly Father, we never wanted to be an "inspiration." We just wanted to be normal. Forgive us for only seeing it as thinly veiled patronization when people say they are "inspired," but also give us your wisdom to know when we can honestly tell someone how very annoying that is. Let all of our words be your words, Lord. *Amen.*

A PRAYER FOR THE INSURANCE COMPANY

Dear Father, when the care we need for our child is tied up in endless mountains of insurance bureaucracy, where are you? Where is your voice in never-ending automated voicemail menus? Where is your perfect will when the specialist we most need to see is out of network? Where is your plan when claims are denied? Help us to make our case for our child. Make ways where there are none. Move mountains when needed. And if you would like to sit on hold with our insurance company for an hour or so while we have a break, we are more than happy to give you the number. *Amen.*

FOR INSTITUTIONAL INCOMPETENCE

Dear God, what is there even to say? We are angry. We are reeling. We are seething. Our child is not a piece of paper to be misplaced or a diagnostic code to be mistyped. Mistakes like these have consequences in real, hurting lives, and we are hurting right now. Help us to remember that all systems are run by imperfect people, and help us to extend them grace. Show us how to vent our anger in appropriate ways (which might not include any of the ways we're thinking about right now, if we're honest). Give us wisdom to know how to move forward from this place, Lord. In your Name, *Amen.*

FOR JERKS

Dear God, we know you made and love everyone on this planet, and that every person is your dear and precious child. But really? We're not seeing it right now. We don't understand. Perhaps you could remind this particular individual of their value as a beloved child of God? So they could then share some of that love with others? At the very least, Lord, remind *us.* Help us to show your love even in the places where we don't receive it. Even with the people who make us furious. *Amen.*

FOR THOSE WHO HAVE GONE BEFORE US

Heavenly Father, we thank you for all those whose work paved the way for us to have the accommodations we need in our world today. Thank you for the trailblazers who went before us: Thank you for Thomas Hopkins Gallaudet, Samuel Gridley Howe, Ann Greenberg, Timothy Nugent, and Joni Eareckson Tada. Thank you for the countless mothers and fathers and sisters and brothers and friends who fought for the rights of children so very much like our own. Help us not forget, Lord, the sacrifices that were made for us to have accommodations today. And help us as we continue the charge so that every child, everywhere, can be fully and completely accepted. *Amen.*

5

CHANGES

Have I not commanded you? Be strong and courageous. Do not be terrified; do not be discouraged, for the Lord your God will be with you wherever you go.

Joshua 1:9

JUMPING OUT
THE WINDOW

*E*verything is changing.

My middle son comes home from school and immediately launches into a five-alarm tantrum: we don't have the particular snack he wants, or his sister borrowed his bike helmet, or he lost his page in his book, or he thinks someone touched one of his fuzzy blankets. The details seem ancillary, blending together into an ever-lengthening litany of wrongs, which he recites in ever-escalating volumes. All is not right in his world.

Today, he plunks down on the couch in the living room and demands that everyone else vacate the premises immediately. No one is allowed to be in the living room, or the dining room, or the kitchen, he says. I explain to him that he is welcome to sit on the couch, but that other people need afterschool snacks and a place to do their homework and access to the front door, so we cannot meet his demands that we all leave.

"But this is my calm-down couch!" he screams at me. "I need to calm down!"

"No one is arguing that you need to calm down," I tell him. "But this is not your calm-down couch."

I try to reason with him, pointing out that the busiest room in the house is not a logical place for solitude. But he can't hear me. I can't get to his rational side. He is already too far gone.

Because everything is changing. And change is hard.

When his older brother started middle school this year, I knew it was going to be a significant transition for my son. He adores his big brother—although he often struggles to express his affection in appropriate ways—and I worried that this transition would upend him. Suddenly his beloved brother has a shared campus with his big sister, with shared teachers, shared references, shared in-jokes, and he is left out of their world.

We disassemble the toddler bed for our youngest, and for the first time in over a decade our house no longer has a crib mattress. Babies do not live here anymore. Our youngest son is thrilled with his new "big boy bed" on the bottom bunk, but for our middle son, this too is a change he cannot weather.

I travel for work twice in the space of two months, and my son can't handle it. Although my husband travels for work regularly, my son isn't used to me being the one who goes away. And it unravels him.

Finally, with impeccable timing, I get an email from the school saying that my son's aide has requested not to work with him anymore. Effective immediately.

• • •

My middle son comes home from school and immediately launches into another five-alarm tantrum. Today it's the snack choices again, or maybe his shirt suddenly feels too tight, or he can't untie his shoes. Whatever the culprit, the tantrum escalates until he grabs the iron from the ironing board and throws it at me. He misses, which only increases his rage, but the iron's plastic casing shatters as it hits the floor, and my youngest son bursts into tears. I put my hands on my middle son's shoulders and guide him to his room.

"It's okay to be angry," I tell him. "It's okay to be very, *very* angry. But we do not throw things in our anger."

I tell him to stay in his room until he calms down.

I go back downstairs to pick up the broken iron, comfort my youngest son, and get my other children ready for homework and afterschool activities, all with the corner of my eye on my middle son's door. Maybe he'll stay in his room until he calms down, and maybe he won't. I'm picking up plastic shards when, suddenly, my middle son is standing in the living room again, still screaming at me. And I don't understand how he got there. His door is still closed. I wonder for a moment if I am losing my mind—until I notice my son is limping, and I realize what has happened.

He kicked the screen out of his second-story window and jumped off the porch overhang to the ground. Because he was angry, and he has zero impulse control when he's angry.

My younger daughter needs me to drive her to dance class. My older daughter needs her music for her harp lesson. My oldest son needs help with his vocabulary homework. My youngest son is crying on the floor surrounded by pieces of a broken iron. And my middle son just jumped out a second-story window.

I'm not sure I can do this anymore.

All the services in the world will never fill the gaps, the places in our days and lives when it is just me—and my four other children—trying to navigate our world as best we can while helping my son navigate his.

• • •

"My ankles hurt," my son says later that night.

I respond before I can catch myself: "Ya *think*?"

He has calmed down, but I have not. Eventually he deigned to eat a less-preferred snack, or found the page in his book, or decided that his blanket didn't smell like his sister touched it. And he is now okay. Curled up on the couch under his fuzzy blanket while the family buzzes around him, he reads to himself and is content. The wrongs in his world have been righted. But the wrongs in my world remain. I watch him read while I help my oldest son with his vocabulary.

"Admonish," my son says.

"To warn," I automatically reply. "To caution against. 'I *admonished* your brother to never, ever jump out of a window again.'"

"How come you always know these words right away?"

"Because I'm a writer."

"Irate," my son continues.

"Angry," I say. "Very angry. 'Your brother got so *irate* that he jumped out a window.'"

My son gives me a look. "Predispose," he says.

"To make more likely, or susceptible," I reply. "'The way your brother's brain is wired makes him *predisposed* to doing things like jumping out a window.'"

"You seem a little fixated on that," my son says.

"I *am*. He jumped out of the window. He freaking *defenestrated* himself."

"That's not one of our words this week, Mom."

I look at my middle son, reading on the couch, and a thousand what-ifs both present and future chase one another around and around in my mind. What if he'd been seriously injured? What if he does it again? What should I tell the school? What happens when, someday, his anger explodes while he's driving a car or at his work or in the presence of the police? What then? I feel a cold slick of dread inside me. I just want to wrap my son up in all of his fuzzy blankets and keep him safe forever. I don't want anything to ever change.

PRAYERS

For a Transition

When you spoke this world into existence, Lord, you created order and routine. And you said that it was good. In our broken and fallen state, all creation is crying over the loss of that order. Transitions are hard; change sometimes seems impossible. Disruptions in our routine throw us into chaos. Be with us, Lord, in this coming change. Breathe your peace into our terror and show us the hope of a redeemed world, where your perfect design always prevails. *Amen.*

For Fear

Father God, we have been afraid before, but we have never felt fear like this. This is a fear that wakes us in the middle of the night, and clenches our stomachs with its fists. This is a fear that shrouds us during the day and doesn't let us go. Be present with us, God. Be with us in our deepest fears. Be stronger than our fear. Vanquish our fear with your love. *Amen.*

WHEN STARTING MEDICATION

Father of all, you tell us that all of our needs are met in you. But sometimes we're confused about what that means. We are trusting in your provision now through the use of medication. We are grateful for the knowledge of the medical and psychiatric communities that have made this choice a possibility, and we entrust the outcome to you. Give us the wisdom we need; help us know if this is a good fit; help our care providers listen well to our feedback. Guide us on this step of our journey, Lord. *Amen.*

FOR A MEDICATION CHANGE

God, we come to you both excited and scared. We are excited about the possibility of finding a medication that might better suit our needs, but we are scared about the change. In this time of transition, remind us that you are closer than our very heartbeats and intimately involved in every detail of our lives. Remind us that you care. Give us insight into our own needs and the ability to communicate those needs to others. In Jesus' Name, *Amen.*

FOR A NEW AIDE

Lord, we thank you for your gifts that allow people to understand us and help us. We pray for our new aide, [Name], that you will give [him/her] the wisdom to discern our needs, to accompany us on our path, and to gently lead us into our fullest potential. We pray that this aide will be a good match, that the seeds of this new relationship would flourish into trust, and that through all of this you would stay by our side. *Amen.*

When Moving to a New House

Lord, we thank you for the opportunity to move to a new house! We're excited and happy, and we also fear this change in routine as we mourn the loss of our familiar place. Be with us in our new space, Lord. Make it feel like the place we belong; make it truly our home. *Amen.*

For the Loss of Family Employment

God of all we need, we come to you in fear. The provision you have given our family has been taken away. Without employment we cannot sustain this family, let alone care for our child. Be with us now, Lord. Make a way where we see no way. Help us in the overwhelming tasks of securing stop-gap solutions until we can find permanent employment again. And please, make that day come quickly. *Amen.*

A Celebration of a Milestone

Father of the universe, we come to you today rejoicing! Our child [Name] has achieved [a milestone]—and we are so grateful. When we feel left out of other people's celebrations, remind us that we, too, have our own milestones to commemorate. Thank you for each treasured one. In your holy Name, *Amen.*

For a Graduation

God of the universe, you gave us signs and seasons by which to mark the passage of time. Today we mark that passage with a celebration! Bless [Name] as [he/she] graduates. Thank you for the time spent in this place, for the memories and the blessings and the growth we experienced. Be with us in this new phase of life, in the excitement and the uncertainty that this change brings. Help [Name] to feel special and celebrated today, Lord. In your Name, *Amen.*

FOR TRANSITION TO ASSISTED/RESIDENTIAL LIVING

Lord, we ask your blessing on our child [Name], who is transitioning into a residential living program. Thank you for the opportunities presented there. Be with our child every moment of the day, as so many of those moments will now be without us. Comfort us in our child's absence. Comfort our child as [he/she] makes the adjustment to this new home. Thank you for the dedicated staff who will help care for our child. We pray for safety, assurance, and peace. May this be a place where our child knows your love. *Amen.*

FOR OUR CHILD'S EMPLOYMENT

God of all, we thank you that our child is able to work. We thank you for both the opportunity and the challenge that work will surely bring. Be with [Name] each day. Surround this work environment with safety, and may [Name] find both growth and delight in the work. In all our working and our resting, may we always remember that you are our provider. *Amen.*

FOR GROWING UP

Lord, we thank you for the life you have given to [Name]. We thank you that as [Name] grows, [he/she] carries your light into this world. We thank you for those you've allowed to see that light in [him/her]. Bless [Name] throughout [his/her] life; keep [him/her] ever close to you. And no matter what the future holds, we rest in the knowledge that you are ever holding [Name] in the same hands that hold up the sky. We love you, Lord. *Amen.*

6

SEASONS OF THE YEAR

Praise be to the name of God for ever and ever;
wisdom and power are his.
He changes times and seasons;
he sets up kings and deposes them.
He gives wisdom to the wise
and knowledge to the discerning
He reveals deep and hidden things;
he knows what lies in darkness,
and light dwells with him.

DANIEL 2:20-22

THE CORN MAZE

*I*t's a brilliant blue day and we're on our way to a corn maze with my brother, his wife, and their three kids. I'm feeling jubilant—it has been a hard week for my middle son, but he loves this annual pilgrimage to the corn maze, and he has been talking about it, as he does every year, for weeks. As outings go, it's a good fit: we're outdoors, with limited crowds, trying to solve a puzzle in the form of a maze. And he loves all things farm-related—open space, animals, and (as he frequently reminds me) the smell of manure. All the ingredients for a successful time are here.

And yet.

Things start to turn south not long after we enter the maze. My son wants to be the one and only map reader. He doesn't want to wait his turn to make a "rubbing" of each goalpost in the corn maze. He doesn't like the pencils we were given to make the rubbings, as they don't have erasers. And did I mention he wants to be the only person reading the map?

Then, "I'm thirsty!" he yells. "Where's my water bottle?"

A quick scan of backpacks and coat pockets reveals that the water bottles, somehow, were inadvertently left in the car. My son roars. "I'M THIRSTY! I NEED A DRINK RIGHT NOW!" Another family appears around a bend in the path, spots my son, and decides not to turn our way.

I'm not sure what to do. It's not a question of simply popping back to the car and grabbing the water bottles—we are, after all, literally lost in a cornfield. I comment to that effect.

"A cornfield that we *paid* for the privilege of getting lost in," my brother says, as he does every year. "Why do we keep doing this? How is this fun?"

"We do this because the kids love it," I say, as I've said every year before. I secretly suspect my husband loves it, too, for reasons I can't quite fathom. Maybe it has to do with being lost but not having to ask for directions? Because being lost is the whole point?

I watch the eight cousins, laughing and traipsing through the maze together. That is . . . seven cousins. One cousin is now sitting on the ground and screaming.

• • •

When my son was five, he became obsessed with a story in a children's magazine given to us by a friend about the birth of a baby longhorn.

"Read me baby longhorns!" he would call. Even though he could read the story himself, he'd ask me to read it to him—over and over and over again. It was a fact-based nonfiction piece, and at one point, I knew far more than I ever wanted to know about birthing cattle: how the cow gives birth, how the calf can stand only moments after being born, how the longhorns will grow.

But my son's favorite line in the story was this: "The mother longhorn nuzzles her baby."

"Nuzzle nuzzle," he would say. "Nuzzle nuzzle."

One day, when we got to this favorite line, he leaned over and rubbed his head against mine.

"Nuzzle nuzzle," he said.

And I started to see why he loved this story. Nestled among the facts and figures he so easily relates to is a short, one-line description of the bond of love between a mother and her child. Maybe surrounded by facts and figures, this is a love he can accept. A love that doesn't overwhelm him quite as much.

"Nuzzle nuzzle, baby longhorn," I said back to him, rubbing my head against his.

• • •

Frustration and compassion chase each other around my heart as I look at my son, sitting on the ground, his arms now wrapped around his legs and his head on his knees. I'm frustrated that he can't snap out of it. I'm frustrated that people are staring at us. I'm frustrated that he had been looking forward to this day and now he can't even enjoy it. He loves being outdoors. He loves walks and mazes and farms and farm animals. This should have worked for him. And I'm flooded with sadness when he can't enjoy the things he loves. But he just can't let things go—the map, the pencil, the water bottle, the way he's already decided in his mind how everything should be.

I don't know if longhorns are actually stubborn, but they *look* stubborn. Raising a creature with two-foot horns sticking out of its head just looks hard. And raising this baby longhorn of mine sometimes seems beyond what I can do.

Frustration and compassion tug and dance.

I ask myself, Why am I frustrated with my son for behaviors he most likely can't control? Is it the "most likely" part that trips me up, complicates my compassion? The fact that I'll never know what is actually within his ability to manage and when (as I asked his IEP team) he's just being a little stinker?

I look at him, sitting in the dirt. He had really been looking forward to this day. And now he's miserable.

Compassion wins.

I squat down beside him, balancing on the balls of my feet to keep my jeans out of the mud. "I'm so sorry about the water bottles," I tell him. "And I'm sorry about the map. And the pencils."

"I'm a good map reader," I hear him say to his knees. "I should be the one to read the map."

"You are, buddy, you are," I say. I pause. Is this the moment to talk again about sharing and taking turns, about flexible thinking and how we don't always get our own way? I decide it's not.

"Maybe today just wasn't a good day," I say instead.

I take a deep breath. We're surrounded by so many things he loves. But something in his brain is keeping him from accessing the joy, just like the same things in his brain keep him from fully accessing the curriculum in school. At school, he has an entire special education team helping him bridge the gap. Here, it's just me.

"I love you, baby longhorn," I tell him. "Nuzzle nuzzle."

"SHUT UP!" he screams at me. "I HATE YOU!"

And we hang in the balance. Will he be able to rally and pull himself together, or will he not? Will we finish the corn maze he's been talking about for weeks, or will I blaze a path through the seven-foot stalks and drag him back to the car? Will we end the day with pizza at our cousins' house, or will we drive home with him hungry and screaming?

I don't know. Sometimes every day, every moment with him feels like a roll of the dice.

I think of a conversation I once had with our family therapist, when I was having a really bad day. A day that couldn't be saved. A day that went irretrievably south.

"But there will be another day. And another try," she said.

"What if I don't want to try again?" I asked. "What if I would rather just quit?"

"I guess you could quit," she said, "but knowing you, I don't think you will."

She's right. I won't quit. I take another deep breath, rearrange myself so I'm fully sitting in the dirt beside my son, and begin another try with my baby longhorn.

PRAYERS

For the New Year

O God who makes all things new, thank you for giving us this new year. We don't know what the year holds—for our child or for us—but we thank you for the opportunity to be in this world together. Bless us, Lord, now and always. *Amen.*

For a Birthday

Lord, we thank you for [Name's] birthday! We thank you for [Name], and we thank you that you brought this child into our lives. May [he/she] grow in ways that delight us this year; may we never lose sight of the fact that each milestone is a miracle from you. Above all, Lord, bless [Name] today. May your comfort and love be present in precious and tangible ways. Keep [him/her] always wrapped securely in your tender arms of love. *Amen.*

For Spring

God of creation, of growth and life, thank you for renewal in your world. Thank you that you are making all things new, both in the created world and in the life of our child. As the days warm and lengthen, give us time to spend outside, give us moments to feel joy and see beauty. Teach us to take delight in the amazing intricacies of everything you have made. *Amen.*

FOR SUMMER

Lord, we thank you for this season of summertime. We pray your blessing on the changes in our routine, and your strength as we seek out the services and structures that will best support our child. Give us wisdom to navigate this time, and an awareness of how the rhythms of the year ever point to you. Thank you that you love our child, Lord. *Amen.*

FOR CAMPS

Lord, we thank you for the ability to go to camp. We thank you for the countless minds and hearts that have made this possibility a reality for our child. Bless the camp staff, Lord—bless the directors and the counselors, the support staff and the volunteers. Thank you for an opportunity that, at one point, we wouldn't have had. Go with our child [Name] each day, Lord. Help [him/her] to adjust to the camp environment, to have fun, and to meet you in the wonder of your creation. *Amen.*

FOR FALL

Lord, as the days grow shorter and colder, help us find you in the crunch of leaves, the chill in the air, the turning of the seasons. As we begin our fall activities, Lord, thank you for all the places where our child is welcomed and accepted. Help us to flourish in these spaces, both the ones we return to at this time every year, and the ones that are new. Be with us always, Lord. *Amen.*

FOR WINTER

O God of warmth, be our warmth this winter. Keep us safe on slippery roads and sidewalks; protect us from illnesses that fester in cold winter months. You know, Lord, all the ways that winter is just a little bit harder for us. Be with us in those places. Thank you for warm houses and schools and places of worship, for all the spaces where we gather during these months. Show us your beauty in the crystals of snowflakes and the reflected light of icicles; show us your beauty in the ways our child sees winter. Thank you for giving us signs and seasons to illuminate different facets of yourself. *Amen.*

FOR CHRISTMAS

O God of promise, on this day we remember how you wrapped your own son in frail flesh to come to this earth and be with us. Your perfect son came to reveal your love, in the most unexpected of ways. Thank you that you still reveal your love in unexpected ways; thank you for the ways you show us your love through the life of our child. In the busyness and chaos of Christmas Day, point us back to you, to the wonder and miracle of a stable stall where love became incarnate. Help us to remember that, at the end of the day, all that matters is you. *Amen.*

FOR HOLIDAYS

Lord, we thank you for this holiday. We thank you that you have given us signs and seasons, days of feasting and of celebration.

We also ask your guidance as we navigate this holiday with our child [Name]. As schedules are disrupted, as demands increase, and as frustrations and exhaustion rise, remind us, Lord, that you are the reason we celebrate. Help us always remember that we can turn to you for rest, even in the midst of celebration. Thank you, Lord. *Amen.*

FOR THE SUNRISE

God of the morning, we thank you for this new day. Thank you for the sun that lights and warms our world. Be with us in the challenges and joys of this day, so that when we feel like we can't go on, we remember: the sun will rise again. And your love will carry us through. *Amen.*

FOR THE SUNSET

God of the evening, thank you for the colors you splash across the sky to bid us goodnight. Thank you for this day, Lord, for another opportunity to serve you as we raise this child you gave us. Thank you for the moments when we saw your hands at work today, and grant us peaceful rest this night. *Amen.*

FOR SPECIAL TRADITIONS

God of our fathers and mothers, we thank you for traditions. Thank you for the many moments of significance that bring meaning to our lives, touchstones that point us to you. Help us navigate this tradition today, Lord. Help us find ways to make it accessible for our child, so that all who participate may feel loved and included. Thank you for our family, Lord. *Amen.*

FOR TRAVELING

Holy Father, traveling is a nightmare. To all the usual stressors and annoyances, we're adding the complications of traveling with our child. Give us unmeasured grace as we do so. Put the people in our path who need to be there; keep far, far away those who don't. Shelter us as we move through changing spaces, and give us rest at the end of each day—the sweet, uncomplicated rest that only you can provide. Make memories with us today. In your Name, *Amen.*

FOR A TIME CHANGE

Dear God, *why?* We know this terrible idea was originally intended to make our lives better, and maybe it had something to do with cows? But we hate it. Our entire routine is going to be thrown into chaos—we will eat at the wrong time, sleep at the wrong time (or not at all), and you know the effects will ripple out for days if not weeks. As we turn our clocks, turn our hearts toward you. Or, really, just move in the hearts of the powers that be to do away with time changes already. *Amen.*

A BLESSING FOR VISITING FAMILY

O Lord, this is complicated. You know how we long to see relationships nurtured between our family and our child—and you know how difficult this can be too. Make this visit a moment of blessing and not of stress. Give everyone charitable spirits, willing hearts, and the ability to receive not just what is being said but what is meant. Surround us with your mercy. Thank you for all the many people you've put in our child's life. Help us communicate how best to love your child [Name]. In Jesus' Name, *Amen.*

FOR HOPE

God of hope, we come to You with outstretched hands.
When our hearts feel sick with longing,
Give us hope.
When our eyes can't see the clearing,
Give us hope.
When our feet are tired from falling,
Give us hope.
When our hands are numb from reaching,
Give us hope.
Until all our very being is fully found in You,
Give us hope.
In the breaking and the yearning, in our finding and our losing,
and in every step along this pilgrim path, give us hope.
Tend our fragile hearts, Lord. Teach us how to find our hope in You.
Amen.

FOR JOY

God, you surprise us with joy, even in the midst of our sorrow.
Right now, our sorrow is so deep that we cannot find your joy.
But we believe there is joy that is deeper,
Remind us of joy that is deeper,
Stir in us joy that is deeper,
As we turn our whole selves to you.
Amen.

7

THANKSGIVINGS

Give thanks to the Lord, call on his name;
make known among the nations what he has done.
Sing to him, sing praise to him;
tell of all his wonderful acts.
Glory in his holy name;
let the hearts of those who seek the Lord rejoice.
Look to the Lord and his strength;
seek his face always.

1 CHRONICLES 16:8-11

HARRY POTTER GOES
TO CHURCH

I'm kicking around the idea of taking all five of our kids to see our youth pastor's ordination to the priesthood. He is the youth pastor, after all, and he also serves as chaplain of the church's preschool, where our youngest son attends.

But the service is on a Friday night, and will most likely extend beyond bedtime, at the end of a long week two weeks before Christmas. Nothing about this says "good idea." As I ponder, I'm also saddened, as I so often am, at the thought of my middle son sitting in the church library alone, playing Minecraft, while the rest of our family participates in the service.

So I ask my son what he thinks about going. And about maybe trying—just for this one service—to sit with us in the sanctuary.

"Will there be food?" he asks.

"Yes," I say.

"Can I bring Harry Potter?" he asks.

"Yes," I say.

"Okay," he says. "I'll come."

I'm shocked. It was that simple. Then again, maybe I shouldn't be surprised. After all, my son is almost nine-and-three-quarters. And as any Harry Potter aficionado knows, magical things can happen at nine-and-three-quarters.

So we go.

• • •

I've always thought of liturgical churches like ours as places of wonder and magic—not totally unlike Harry Potter. We, too, have ancient-looking robes that billow out behind us as we walk. We, too, have candles and processions and strange-sounding incantations: *Veni Sancte Spiritus* doesn't sound all that different from *Wingardium Leviosa*. Our sanctuary even looks a bit like the Great Hall at Hogwarts, with soaring ceilings and somber tones. And the rich gold-and-scarlet cloth that drapes the high altar at Pentecost could just as easily hang in the common room of Gryffindor.

The seven of us file into a pew toward the back of the church. My son stretches out on his stomach, his elbows propped on my husband's lap, and opens Harry Potter. As the stentorian notes of the organ prelude fade, we stand as a congregation to sing "The Church's One Foundation." My son does not stand. He rolls onto his back and turns a page.

My four-year-old grabs my hand and clambers onto the pew to watch the processional, wide-eyed.

"Dere's Chaplain Ben!" he squeaks as Chaplain Ben walks by, and his squeak earns us a smile and a wave. When the bishop passes our pew, my four-year-old's eyes grow even wider.

"Dat man looks like a *king*!" he says. "But he's carrying a shepherd's crook! Is he a shepherd *and* a king?"

Out of the mouths of babes. I watch the bishop process up to the altar, carrying his shepherd's crook, brocade vestments billowing out behind him like Dumbledore. I motion to my husband to try and get our nine-year-old's attention. My seven-year-old steals all our bulletins so she can draw on them. My four-year-old takes off his shoes and hands them to me.

"I don't want to wear dese shoes anymore," he says conversationally, as he deposits them into my lap. "But if we leave dem here, I will be *piss-ded*."

Where did he learn such reprehensible language? I tuck his shoes alongside the embroidered kneelers and promise him I won't forget.

My seven-year-old wants to know when the actual priest-making is going to take place. "Now?" she whispers incessantly, tugging at my arm. "Now? Now? Now?" My nine-year-old flips a page and sighs, loudly. At the end of the row, my fourteen- and twelve-year-olds scooch slightly farther away. They're probably pretending they don't know us.

As Chaplain Ben is presented for examination, my nine-year-old suddenly closes his book and sits upright.

"Will you be loyal to the doctrine, discipline, and worship of Christ as this church has received them?" the bishop asks. "And will you, in accordance with the canons of this church, obey your bishop and other ministers who may have authority over you and your work?"

"I am willing and ready to do so," Chaplain Ben responds.

Thumb holding his page in Harry Potter, my son is focused, drinking in every word. His blue-gray eyes are trained on the front of the church and his body is taut, as if waiting—perhaps for the Sorting Hat to shout out Chaplain Ben's new House? The service continues, and my son returns to his book.

As the time for Communion draws closer, I start to whisper to him in one-minute intervals the remaining time until I will ask him to close the book. We're well over an hour into this event, after bedtime on a Friday night two weeks before Christmas, and 99 percent of my brain is reminding me that we are living on borrowed time. I should probably just cut my losses, celebrate my victories, skip Communion, and head home. But 1 percent of my brain—maybe it's the desire to make it to the end of the evening? A longing to receive Communion together as a family?—is whispering that we should stay.

I listen to the 1 percent.

As the congregants file from the pews into the aisle, I gently touch my son's shoulder and motion for him to close the book. He grabs a bulletin from my daughter's stack and places it as a bookmark between the pages.

My four-year-old still isn't wearing his shoes, but I decide that's a battle I'm not going to fight. As we walk up the aisle, my nine-year-old launches into his rendition of the "Floss," a dance that involves a lot of synchronized hip-shaking and arm-waving. My husband moves to stop him, but I shake my head. I feel the enchantment of the evening beginning to fade, and I want to hold out until the very last possible moment. I let him dance.

We process up to the altar, shoeless and "flossing." Let the little children come.

The bishop makes his way down the row of kneeling parishioners, distributing the body of Christ, as my family inches closer to the railing. He stops for a moment when he sees us, all seven in a row. Then, as my son drops out of the "Floss" into a flop on the embroidered kneeler at the altar, the bishop himself kneels down, brocade robes spilling onto the hard stone floor around him, and speaks directly to my son.

"Thank you for coming tonight," he says.

My son straightens up, his spine ramrod-straight, and looks the bishop in the eye. I hold my breath.

"I'm thankful for every single person who came to this ordination service tonight," the bishop goes on to say, "and especially all the children." His eyes take in my five little and not-so-little ones, kneeling at the altar, and return again to rest on my son.

"I'm particularly grateful for you," he says.

My son is still holding the bishop's gaze, and I am still holding my breath. Is he thankful for my son because he's a child? Or did he see him "flossing" his way up the aisle?

Did he truly *see* my son?

I think he did. And this shepherd/king knelt down, in his brocade robes, and told my son he is welcome.

And my son heard every word he said.

Following the recessional, I gather up the shoes and the stack of bulletins and the Harry Potter book, and we proceed, joyously, to the promised reception that awaits. For an hour and forty-one minutes on a Friday night, two weeks before Christmas, we did it. Harry Potter, my family, my son, and me.

• • •

We arrive home late, and I plug in the lights on the Christmas tree. My son catapults himself onto the couch and opens his book.

"Oh no you don't, buddy," I say. "It's way past your bedtime."

But part of me just wants to let him sit here, reading, in the twinkling lights of the Christmas tree on this magical night. Our tree is beautiful this year—not like the year when he was six, when he bolted away from us at the Christmas tree farm, found the scrawniest, most Charlie Brown tree on the lot, and promptly named it Fred. And we had to get it. The Year of Fred, we did not have a beautiful tree.

But this year, we do. I think about how we picked out our tree this year, how our son stayed with us and was able to more or less compromise on our selection. That felt, perhaps, like progress. (Then again, he also launched himself through the tree baler in a split second when no one was looking, emerging on the other side all tied up in Christmas tree netting. "We should just leave him like that," his older sister proposed.)

Two steps forward, one step back.

"I've added a new possible occupation to my list of things I might be when I grow up," my son announces from the couch.

"Oh yes?" I say. "And what might that be?"

"I think I might be a priest," he says. I absorb this information.

"I think I would make a good priest," he continues. "I could put my *own* spin on all the stories from the Bible."

I laugh. "I also think you would make a good priest," I tell him, "and here's why. I think you would make a good priest because you wouldn't judge anyone. You would say, 'All, *all*, are welcome here.' Like our bishop. And like him, you would mean it."

"Oh, I would totally do that," he agrees. "I'm, like, the least judgy person I know."

And with that, he scoops up Harry Potter and heads off to bed.

I've been on this carousel too long to think that all of our problems are now solved, that next week and the week after and the week after that my son will sit in the sanctuary and participate, to whatever extent he is able, in the service. I don't even know that this is a "turning point." What I do know is that this service was a good experience at church. And every good experience at church is just that: a good experience at church. I do know that tonight, a man in a gold-and-scarlet robe got down on his knees and told my son that he was welcome.

My older children like to debate what House they would be in, should they ever attend Hogwarts. Would they be Gryffindor, where dwell the brave and true of heart? Or would their bookish brains land them in Ravenclaw? They're crafty and strategic too, so Slytherin isn't out of the question.

When they ask me, I tell them I know exactly what House I would be in. Should my Hogwarts letter ever arrive by owl (and should I suddenly, miraculously, revert to being eleven years old), I know exactly where I would be sorted. Like my kids, I may have the courage of a Gryffindor, the brains of a Ravenclaw, the cunning of a Slytherin—but my house would be Hufflepuff. For what did Helga Hufflepuff say? "I'll teach the lot / And treat them just the same."

Let the little children—*all* the little children—come.

PRAYERS

A Blessing for Parents

God of all love, we thank you for [Name] and [Name], the parents of [Name]. Thank you for bringing this child into their lives. Thank you that this child is your precious creation, and that you will give these parents the grace required to meet [Name's] needs. Give them strength in the day-to-day frustrations, and illuminate their lives with your joy. Help them to remember that you promise to meet all of our needs through Jesus Christ our Lord. Bless this family that you have created, today and always. *Amen.*

A Blessing for Families

God of good gifts, we thank you for the gift of families. Thank you for giving us people to surround us with love, and homes as places of grace and growth. Bless our family's years together, Lord. Bless both our struggles and our moments of joy. Be present in the little things, the daily minutiae that make up our lives together. Give us abundant grace, more than enough for the tasks to which you have called us. Be our every hope, Lord. *Amen.*

A Blessing for Siblings

Dear God, we thank you that you have chosen [Name] to be a part of this family. Bless [his/her] siblings, [Siblings' Names]. Fill their lives together with love. Thank you for the compassion and awareness that will grow in their hearts as they share their lives with [Name]. Give them joyful moments together, and special moments that are theirs alone. Thank you for the ways that being siblings with [Name] will shape them; protect them from any ways that being [his/her] sibling might hurt them. Above all, knit them together in your all-encompassing love. In Jesus' Name, *Amen.*

A Blessing for an Adoption

O God who calls us all your children, thank you for [Name] and [Name], who are preparing to call this child, [Name], their own. Bless the family that is formed here today. Thank you for the love you have given them. Nurture that love as it grows, and surround this family with your light. *Amen.*

A Blessing for Foster Parents

Lord, thank you for the love you have given [Name] and [Name], who are now making room in their lives for a child in need. Bless them, Lord. Bless them through the joys and challenges, the struggles and successes. Give them hope, patience, and bravery. Thank you for their commitment to this child. In your Name, *Amen.*

A Blessing for Good Friends

God of love, bless our friends.

Thank you for all the ways their lives enrich ours.

Protect their families and all those whom they love.

Surround them always with your light.

Amen.

FOR COMPASSION

God of compassion, show us your compassion. Give us compassion for our child [Name]. Give us the grace to see everyone who accompanies us on this journey with your eyes. Help us to inhabit this world in a spirit of gentleness. And give us compassion for ourselves. *Amen.*

FOR SCIENTIFIC DISCOVERY

God of discovery, thank you for the marvels you have worked into the very fabric of this world. Thank you for those who work tirelessly to ease the suffering of your children; thank you for medications, therapies, vaccines. Be with those whose minds you have gifted for these tasks, Lord. Help them see the things that are hidden, and uncover the things you desire for them to find. Protect them as they work, Lord, and protect their work itself, that it might show forth your glory. In your Name, *Amen.*

FOR THERAPISTS AND MENTAL HEALTH PROFESSIONALS

O God of wonder, thank you for creating us with thoughts and emotions, rich and unseen worlds that reflect your very essence. Thank you for the intricacies of the human mind. Thank you for those whom you have skilled in tending and touching our minds, for those who speak hope to our hearts. Bless them in their work,

Lord. Thank you for spaces of safety and trust where we can feel your love and light. *Amen.*

FOR THOSE WHO LOVE US

God of love, thank you for all those who love us.

Thank you for those who laugh with us, cry with us, pray with us.

Thank you for those who understand.

Bless their every moment, Lord.

Surround them with peace.

Give them unbounded joy as they move through this world.

May Your love imbue them with every good gift.

God of love, thank you for all those who love us.

Amen.

FOR THE SPECIAL NEEDS COMMUNITY

Lord, thank you for the people in our lives who "get it." Thank you for those who, with merely a word or a glance, understand. Thank you for a place of respite from constantly having to explain. Thank you for every shared prayer, every affirmation, every partnered step together on this journey. Thank you for the miraculous ways in which you brought us together. Nurture these relationships, Lord. They are priceless. Help us to never take them for granted. In your Name, *Amen.*

A THANKSGIVING FOR ART

Lord, we thank you that in creativity, we mirror you. Thank you for giving us this glimpse into your very nature. Thank you for the people in our lives who bring this gift of creativity to our child. Thank you for the mess of creation, the beauty, the process that is its own reward. *Amen.*

A THANKSGIVING FOR MUSIC

Lord, we thank you for the gift of music. We thank you that music can communicate in ways words cannot; we thank you for the ways that music has touched our child. Thank you for spaces where our child can participate in the glory of music. *Amen.*

A THANKSGIVING FOR DANCE

Lord, we thank you for the gift of dance. We thank you for the way our bodies feel when we move, and we thank you for those in our lives who have brought this gift of movement to our child. In movement, we find your joy and healing. Be with us as we dance our love for you. *Amen.*

A THANKSGIVING FOR BEAUTY

God of beauty, you are beautiful, and we see that beauty in your creation. Thank you for giving us the ability to see that beauty in unexpected places. Slow us down, Lord, as we hurry through this world; help us find the moments of joy and delight you have tucked into this world for us. Teach us to savor the dew on a spider's web and the marvelous whorls of a fingerprint. Teach us to see your beauty unfolding in our child each and every day. Come with us as we search for beauty. Be with us always. *Amen.*

FOR MOMENTS OF DELIGHT

God of infinite delight, thank you for the many ways we see your fingerprints on this world. Help us to not lose sight of the joy and delight you created, both in this earth we inhabit and in the beloved children who dwell here. Show us delight in small and unexpected ways, Lord. Catch us by surprise. We are ready and willing to be amazed by you, today and always. *Amen.*

FOR OUR CHILD

Holy God, you tell us that every good and perfect gift is from above. We thank you for the perfect gift of [Name], and for the honor of having [her/his] life entwined with ours. We pray that you would use us to bless [Name], and we acknowledge and honor all the many ways in which [Name] has blessed us. Thank you, Lord, for choosing us to be the parents of your precious child. We are so grateful. *Amen.*

FOR SPECIAL GRACE

Heavenly Father, before the foundation of the world you chose our child to be a dearly beloved child of yours. We are honored by the privilege of being your hands and feet here on the earth. Thank you for the joys, and for the sorrows. Thank you for the triumphs and the setbacks. Thank you for everything that makes this child a beautiful, priceless creation in your sight. Thank you for the ways you have stretched us and grown us, opening our eyes to see you ever more clearly. Thank you for all the ways you have given us special grace. *Amen.*

OTHER PRAYERS

For a New Mobility Device

Lord, we come to you with excitement and anticipation, as we acquire a [mobility device] for our child. We are grateful that we live in a time where such a thing exists, and we pray you would use it to enhance and enrich [Name's] life. Thank you for the minds and hearts of those who designed this instrument for our benefit. Help us learn to use this tool wisely, to persevere when the adjustment seems difficult, and ultimately to be able to more fully participate in this world you have given us. *Amen.*

For a White Cane

Lord, thank you for the many tools you give us to help us navigate this world. Thank you for this white cane, for the ways it can provide mobility and freedom. Thank you for the pioneers who went before in its creation. As we reach out into your world, give us guidance. Navigate us well. Shield us from all snares and arrows as we take these new steps. In your Name, *Amen.*

For Cochlear Implants

Creator God, when you spoke this world into existence, those sound waves carried life into what had once been a void. The echoes of those sound waves still ring today, but sometimes we can't hear them—just as sometimes we can't see the plans you have for us. Be with [Name] today as [he/she] receives cochlear implants. Guide the surgeon's hands that they may move as your hands, and restore to all of us the echoes of the words of your creation, and glimpses of the plans you have for us. In your Name, *Amen.*

For Sign Language

God who communes with our very souls, thank you for all the ways you've given us to communicate with each other. Thank you for sign language, for giving a way to speak with their hands to those who can't hear. Bless the teachers and interpreters of sign language; bless the families who take on the challenge of a new language to learn to speak with their child. As we shape our hands into words, Lord, hold us always in your hands. *Amen.*

For Braille

God of all understanding, thank you for giving us Braille. Thank you that through this writing, we can read and understand. Thank you for the worlds that are opened to us. Be with those who write and teach in Braille, and bless their work and efforts to bring these worlds to us. *Amen.*

FOR AN EPIPEN

God of all power, we thank you for our EpiPen. Thank you for the jolt like a bolt of lightning, cleaving us from death to life, fear and relief coursing white-hot adrenaline through our veins. Thank you for the minds of those who saw the way to create this lifesaving device. May we never be without it when we need it; may we never be afraid to use it. Be with us, Lord, now and always. *Amen.*

WHEN OUR CHILD HURTS ANOTHER

God our Father, this is a pain we can't bear. Our child has hurt someone. It would be awful enough if our child was the one who was hurt, but somehow this is worse. We feel so many things: embarrassment, failure, sorrow, compassion. Be with us in this moment when we feel so broken. Enfold us in your comfort, Lord. *Amen.*

FOR SOMEONE HURT BY OUR CHILD

Lord, our child has hurt someone. And in our pain, it feels like nothing about this situation can be redeemed. But you are our healer, the One who makes all things new. Redeem this situation, Lord. Breathe forgiveness and restoration where right now we only see hurt and shame. In your Name, *Amen.*

BEFORE A SURGERY

God of healing, be with us as we prepare for surgery. Bless the surgeon's hands, and bless all who work today to help us. Thank you for the medical advances and discoveries that have made today's surgery possible. Heal us, Lord. We put our trust in you. In Jesus' Name, *Amen.*

AFTER A SUCCESSFUL SURGERY

Lord, thank you for a successful surgery. Be with us now as we begin the healing process. Keep us safe from complications, and give us grace and patience during recovery. Thank you for the marvel of the human body, and how we show forth your glory. Be with us, Lord. *Amen.*

AFTER AN UNSUCCESSFUL SURGERY

Dear God, our hearts are breaking. We knew this was a possibility, but we just didn't want to accept it. We don't want to accept it, now. We trusted and prayed . . . and this surgery was still unsuccessful. Help us, Lord. Be with us now as we plan the next steps. Help us not to feel abandoned, but remind us that you are always here, you are holding us . . . every step of the way. *Amen.*

FOR TIME IN THE CAR

Dear God, did you know, when the automobile was first invented, how very much time we'd have to spend in it? We are grateful for the mode of transportation, Lord, but sometimes we're just sick of having so many places to go. Be with us at red lights and wrong turns, in parking lots and on highways. Guide us as we seek out the very best for our child, and give us grace to navigate all the driving that entails. *Amen.*

A THANKSGIVING FOR LEGO BRICKS

Dear Lord, you know how much we hate those little plastic pieces when we step on them barefoot in the middle of the night. Also they clog the vacuum cleaner. But God, we are so thankful for LEGO bricks. Thank you for the minds that designed this toy, for the communities that have grown up around it, and for all the children in those communities that are so very much like ours. Thank you that we don't need social skills to bond over LEGO. Thank you that we can actually build social skills, somewhat organically, while bonding over LEGO bricks. Most of all, Lord, thank you for the joy these little plastic pieces bring to our child. *Amen.*

For Special Olympics

O God who gifted our bodies with so many ways of moving through your world, we thank you for the Special Olympics. We thank you for giving us a place where children like ours can enjoy playing sports. Be with our team and with all teams, Lord. Bless the coaches, the volunteers, and all who work to bring this experience to our child. *Amen.*

For Therapy Animals

Lord, we thank you that all creation shows us aspects of you: your creativity, your joy, your playfulness, your love. Thank you, Lord, for our therapy animal, [Name]. Thank you for the bond between [Name] and our child, and thank you for all that [Name] has brought into our lives. Thank you for the minds and hearts of trainers and educators who poured into this animal's training, so that this companion can pour into our lives now. Bless this relationship, Lord. Bless all our relationships with your creatures. In Jesus' Name, *Amen.*

ACKNOWLEDGMENTS

*W*riting the acknowledgments is my absolute favorite part of writing a book.

I love acknowledgments so much that I've drafted them for books I will most likely never write. And I always read the acknowledgments in other people's books—lists of names that mean nothing to me, people I will never meet—because to someone, those names mean the world. And I love thinking about all the myriad people who help and support us on our journey.

First, to my entire family, whether you are family through birth, adoption, or foster care. Thank you for being in my life.

To my writers' group: Allison Duncan, Amy Knorr, and Christie Purifoy. Thank you for telling me to just write the overdue baby book already. Your friendship and support are tangible, not theoretical; you told me over and over again that, yes, the book would come into being, and when a global pandemic struck right after I signed the contract, you gave me space and time and empty houses in which to write. Thank you. And thank you for never assuming I will know which ones are the weeds. Y'all. The elephants are trumpeting all around.

Heidi Lee and Kim Munday, so many of the stories in this book were already written before the book was even an idea—written in thousands and thousands of emails to you. (Yes, thousands. You know I went and counted.) You have walked every single step of this journey beside me. Your wisdom, knowledge, and occasional snark have upheld me. When you offer to pray for my family, I know that you actually do. I am so grateful for you. Also how have we been talking for three hours?! I just got here. And there is salted caramel pretzel bark in our future.

Bill Gaventa, thank you for introducing me to the Faith Inclusion Network. Karen Jackson, thank you for your hospitality and strategic planning. Jolene Philo, thank you for being a kindred spirit and introducing me to my agent.

Karen Neumair, thank you for the insight and enthusiasm you brought to my book proposal. It's a joy to work with you.

Ethan McCarthy and the team at InterVarsity Press, thank you for seeing a path for this book to make its way into the world. Thank you for flexibility in scheduling when the pandemic sent all five of my children home, and I couldn't find time to write about them in the middle of raising them.

To my son's entire team: What can I even say? We have laughed together, cried together, and somehow made IEP revision meetings something to look forward to (?!). Who even knew that was possible. In particular I'd like to thank Kelly DeMillion, Nicola Salvatico, Kelly Packer, Amanda Ferraioli, Amy White, Edward Jameson, Leslie Beauregard, and Carolyn Shoemaker.

My family has been blessed by so many people who have gone above and beyond to support us. And some have gone *beyond* above and beyond. You have altered the trajectory of our lives and we are better for it. I am eternally grateful to Megan Cullen, Melissa Driscoll, Laura Harting, and Jill Hughes.

And to my children. If I got to pick my kids from the Little Kid Store, you know I would pick each and every one of you. Today, tomorrow, and always. I could not be grateful enough for your presence in my life. Thank you for being exactly who God made you to be. Thank you for the special privilege of being your mom. I love you.

LIST OF PRAYERS

1. BEGINNINGS
For an Initial Diagnosis, 16
For Decisions, 16
For Testing, 17
A Prayer for a Prenatal Diagnosis, 17
In Times of Fear, 17
When Frustrated, 17-18
A Prayer for Exhaustion, 18
For Never-Ending Mountains of
   Paperwork, 18
When Faced with Uncertainty, 18-19
When God Doesn't Heal, 19
For Grace to Keep Going, 19

2. FAMILY LIFE
For Home Life, 30
For Parents, 30-31
For Siblings, 31
For Extended Family, 31
For Grace in Housework, 31-32
For Mealtime, 32
For Understanding Employers, 32
A Prayer for the Morning, 32-33
A Prayer for the Middle of the Night, 33
For Comfort, 33

A Prayer Before a Home Visit, 33-34
For Respite Care, 34
For a Setback, 34
A Prayer for a Loved One Who Is Out
   of Control, 34-35
A Prayer for a Meltdown, 35
Another Prayer for a Meltdown, 35
A Prayer for Strength, 35
When We Feel Like We're Failing, 35-36
A Prayer for When Everything Seems to
   Be Going Wrong, 36
Another Prayer for When Everything
   Seems to Be Going Wrong, 36
One More Prayer for When Everything
   Seems to Be Going Wrong, 36
When We Want to Quit, 37

3. SCHOOL
At the Start of the School Year, 46
A Blessing for the First Day of School,
   46-47
For Riding the Bus, 47
For Bus Drivers, 47
For Teachers, 48
For Special Education Teachers, 48

For an Aide, 48
For a Substitute Teacher, 49
For a Difficult Teacher/Aide, 49
For Bullying, 49-50
For Bullies, 50
For a Field Trip, 50
Before an IEP Meeting, 50-51
Before Another IEP Meeting, 51
Before Yet Another IEP Meeting, 51

4. Public Life

A Prayer Before Going Out, 60
A Prayer for Being "That Family," 60
For Discrimination, 61
For Accommodation, 61
A Prayer for a Public Scene, 61-62
For Mobile Therapists, 62
For Friends, 62
For the Church, 62
When People Spiritualize Disability, 63
When People Look at Us Funny, 63
Another Prayer for when People Look at Us Funny, 63
When People Say Really Dumb Things, 63-64
When People are "Inspired" by Us, 64
A Prayer for the Insurance Company, 64
For Institutional Incompetence, 64-65
For Jerks, 65
For Those Who Have Gone Before Us, 65

5. Changes

For a Transition, 74
For Fear, 74
When Starting Medication, 75
For a Medication Change, 75
For a New Aide, 75
When Moving to a New House, 76
For the Loss of Family Employment, 76
A Celebration of a Milestone, 76

For a Graduation, 76-77
For Transition to Assisted/Residential Living, 77
For Our Child's Employment, 77
For Growing Up, 77-78

6. Seasons of the Year

For the New Year, 86
For a Birthday, 86
For Spring, 86-87
For Summer, 87
For Camps, 87
For Fall, 87-88
For Winter, 88
For Christmas, 88
For Holidays, 88-89
For the Sunrise, 89
For the Sunset, 89
For Special Traditions, 89
For Traveling, 90
For a Time Change, 90
A Blessing for Visiting Family, 90-91
For Hope, 91
For Joy, 91

7. Thanksgivings

A Blessing for Parents, 102
A Blessing for Families, 102
A Blessing for Siblings, 103
A Blessing for an Adoption, 103
A Blessing for Foster Parents, 103
A Blessing for Good Friends, 103-4
For Compassion, 104
For Scientific Discovery, 104
For Therapists and Mental Health Professionals, 104-5
For Those Who Love Us, 105
For the Special Needs Community, 105
A Thanksgiving for Art, 105-6
A Thanksgiving for Music, 106

A Thanksgiving for Dance, 106
A Thanksgiving for Beauty, 106
For Moments of Delight, 107
For Our Child, 107
For Special Grace, 107

OTHER PRAYERS

For a New Mobility Device, 108
For a White Cane, 108
For Cochlear Implants, 109

For Sign Language, 109
For Braille, 109
For an EpiPen, 110
When Our Child Hurts Another, 110
For Someone Hurt by Our Child, 110
Before a Surgery, 110
After a Successful Surgery, 111
After an Unsuccessful Surgery, 111
For Time in the Car, 111
A Thanksgiving for LEGO Bricks, 111-12
For Special Olympics, 112
For Therapy Animals, 112